Great Misadventures

Great Misadventures

Bad Ideas That Led to Big Disasters

PEGGY SAARI

EDITED BY BETZ DES CHENES

VOLUME ONE: EXPLORATION AND ADVENTURE

AN IMPRINT OF GALE

Detroit • London

Great Misadventures:
Bad Ideas That Led to Big Disasters

Peggy Saari

Staff

Elizabeth Des Chenes, *U·X·L Senior Editor*
Carol DeKane Nagel, *U·X·L Managing Editor*
Thomas L. Romig, *U·X·L Publisher*

Margaret Chamberlain, *Permissions Specialist (Pictures)*

Mary Beth Trimper, *Production Director*
Evi Seoud, *Assistant Production Manager*
Deborah Milliken, *Production Assistant*

Cynthia Baldwin, *Product Design Manager*
Michelle Dimercurio, *Art Director*
Linda Mahoney, *Typesetting*

Library of Congress Cataloging-in-Publication Data

Great Misadventures: Bad Ideas That Led to Big Disasters/ Peggy Saari, editor
    v. cm.
    Includes bibliographical references.
    Summary: Explores 100 historical, political, military, and social events
where human error has led to disaster.
    ISBN 0-7876-2798-4 (set: alk. paper). — ISBN 0-7876-2799-2 (v. 1: alk.
paper) — ISBN 0-7876-2800-X (v. 2: alk. paper) — ISBN 0-7876-2801-8 (v. 3:
alk paper) — ISBN 0-7876-2802-6 (v. 4: alk. paper)
    1. History—Miscellanea—Juvenile literature. 2. Disasters—Juvenile litera-
ture. [1. Disasters. 2. History—Miscellanea]
    I. Saari, Peggy.
    D24 G64 1998
    904—dc21   98-13811
                                                                    CIP

™ This book is printed on acid-free paper that meets the minimum requirements
of American National Standard for information Sciences—Permanence Paper
for Printed Library Materials, ANSI Z39.48-1984.

Printed in the United States of America

10 9 8 7 6 5 4 3 2 1

Contents

Reader's Guide

Great Misadventures: Bad Ideas That Led to Big Disasters presents 100 stories of human error, greed, and poor judgment that span history from ancient times through the present. Each entry, whether on an infamous adventure, a technological failure, a deadly battle, or a social calamity, offers historical background and a vivid description of the event, together with a discussion about why the misadventure is significant.

In many cases, a misadventure had a positive outcome—laws were enacted, failure led to progress, the protagonist became a national hero—but in others, death or destruction were the only result. It is disillusioning to learn, for example, that a great explorer committed atrocities, or that a well-known celebrity was a liar. It is equally disturbing to discover that incompetent leaders caused needless loss of life in wars, or that cutting-edge technology was sometimes useless or even dangerous. The goal of Great Misadventures is to show that success can also involve failure, triumph can encompass defeat, and human beings are inspired by self-interest as often as they are motivated by selflessness.

Format

The Great Misadventures entries are arranged chronologically within four subject volumes: Exploration and Adventure, Science and Technology, Military, and Society. Cross references direct users to related entries throughout the four-volume set, while sources for further reference at the end of each entry offer more information on featured people and events. Call-out boxes present biographical profiles and fascinating facts, and more than 220 black-and-white photographs, illustrations, and maps help illuminate the text. Each volume contains an annotated table of contents, a timeline of important events, and a cumulative index.

Comments and Suggestions

We welcome your comments and suggestions for subjects to feature in future editions of *Great Misadventures*. Please write: Editors, *Great Misadventures*, U•X•L, 27500 Drake Rd., Farmington Hills, Michigan, 48331–3535; call toll-free: 800–877–4253; or fax 1–800–414–5043.

Timeline

415 B.C. Athenian naval commander Alcibiades is defeated during an assault on Syracuse.

325 B.C. Macedonian leader Alexander the Great leads a tragic expedition across the Gedrosia desert.

30 B.C. Egyptian queen Cleopatra commits suicide.

1118 French philosopher Peter Abelard begins a tragic love affair with his student Hëloise.

1187 Christian Crusaders lose the Battle of Hattin to the Muslims.

1212 Stephen of Cloyes, a French shepherd boy, leads the ill-fated Children's Crusade.

1498 Italian explorer Christopher Columbus begins his rule of Hispaniola.

c. 1500 The Norse settlement in Greenland is abandoned.

1533 Spanish conquistador Pedro de Alvarado leads a disastrous trek across the Andes.

1541 Spanish conquistador Francisco Vázquez de Coronado fails to find the Seven Cities of Cibola.

214 B.C	1215	1455
Great Wall of China is built	Magna Carta is written	War of the Roses begins

250 B.C.   1100   1300   1500

1591 English colonists disappear from the Roanoke settlement.

1597 Dutch explorer Willem Barents dies in a failed attempt to find a northeast sea passage to Asia.

1605 English Roman Catholics fail to blow up Parliament as part of the Gunpowder Plot.

1618 English explorer Sir Walter Raleigh is beheaded for disobeying King James I.

1625 The British fleet is defeated in a disastrous misadventure at the port of Cádiz, Spain.

1687 French explorer René-Robert de La Salle is killed by his own men.

1709 The Swedish army loses the Battle of Poltava because of a squabble between two of its commanders.

1776 Hessian colonel Johann Gottlieb Rall loses the Battle of Trenton when he underestimates rebel troop strength.

1779 English explorer James Cook is murdered by angry Hawaiian islanders.

1806 Scottish explorer Mungo Park drowns during an expedition on the Niger River.

1811 Rebellious English textile workers calling themselves "Luddites" begin a failed uprising against the Industrial Revolution.

1812 Poor leadership by American general William Hull leads to the Fall of Detroit during the War of 1812.

1815 French leader Napoléon Bonaparte is defeated by British forces at the Battle of Waterloo.

1831 African American slave Nat Turner leads the failed Southampton Insurrection.

1618
Thirty Years'
War begins

1770
The
Enlightenment
ends

1805
Lewis and Clark
reach the
Pacific Ocean

1600   1700   1800

1844 Canadian trapper Peter Skene Ogden explores territory for Britain that is later lost to the United States in a land dispute.

1846 Donner Party members resort to cannibalism after being trapped in the Sierra Nevada.

1847 British explorer John Franklin is lost at sea during his search for the Northwest Passage.

1855 Deprivations during the Crimean War lead to an overwhelming number of deaths among British soldiers.

1859 Abolitionist John Brown stages a failed raid on the federal arsenal at Harpers Ferry, Virginia.

1861 Australian explorers Robert O'Hara Burke and William John Wills starve to death during their transcontinental expedition.

1863 Confederate general George Edward Pickett marches his troops to certain death at the Battle of Gettysburg.

1863 The African American 54th Massachusetts Regiment stages an heroic but unsuccessful assault on Fort Wagner, South Carolina.

1870 Paraguay's male population is reduced by almost ninety percent during the "War of the Triple Alliance."

1873 British missionary and explorer David Livingstone dies during his final adventure in Africa.

1873 French explorer Francis Garnier makes a tactical error that ends French control of the Vietnamese city of Hanoi.

1876 The 7th Cavalry is annihilated by Sioux and Cheyenne warriors at the Battle of Little BigHorn.

1881 American explorer George Washington De Long and his crew are lost while attempting to find a route to the North Pole through the Bering Strait.

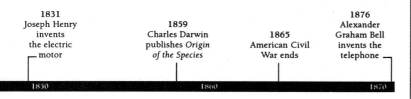

1831
Joseph Henry invents the electric motor

1859
Charles Darwin publishes *Origin of the Species*

1865
American Civil War ends

1876
Alexander Graham Bell invents the telephone

1850   1860   1870

1908 American explorer Frederick Albert Cook claims to be the first man to reach the North Pole.

1911 One hundred and forty-six immigrant workers perish in the Triangle Shirtwaist Company fire in New York City.

1912 British explorer Robert Falcon Scott and his party freeze to death on their return trip from the South Pole.

1912 The luxury ocean liner *Titanic* sinks after hitting an iceberg.

1915 Poor leadership and bad communication leads to high Allied casualties at the Battle of Gallipoli.

1916 Irish revolutionaries stage the unsuccessful Easter Rising.

1919 A steel tank containing 12,000 tons of molasses bursts open in Boston, Massachusetts, and kills twenty-one people.

1919 British troops kill 379 unarmed Indian protestors during the Amritsar Massacre.

1920 Seven Chicago White Sox players are banned from playing baseball for their role in the "Black Sox" betting scandal.

1928 Italian pilot Umberto Nobile crashes the airship *Italia* during a flight to the North Pole.

1934 The Dionne quintuplets are born in Canada and soon become a tourist and media attraction.

1937 American aviator Amelia Earhart and her navigator Fred Noonan are lost on a flight across the Pacific Ocean.

1937 The airship *Hindenberg* explodes after landing in Lakehurst, New Jersey.

1938 The *War of the Worlds* radio broadcast about a fictional Martian invasion causes widespread public panic.

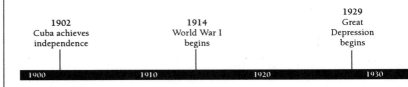

1902 Cuba achieves independence	1914 World War I begins	1929 Great Depression begins

| 1900 | 1910 | 1920 | 1930 |

1941 German leader Adolf Hitler launches Operation Barbarossa, his failed invasion of Russia.

1944 The Japanese navy and air force stage a futile kamikaze attack at the Battle of Leyte Gulf.

1947 American inventor Howard Hughes flies his *Spruce Goose* seaplane for ninety seconds.

1950 U.S. senator Joseph McCarthy launches his four-year search for Communist infiltrators.

1951 U.S. general Douglas MacArthur is relieved of his command during the Korean War.

1953 Julius and Ethel Rosenberg become the first U.S. citizens to be executed for espionage.

1956 A United Airlines DC-7 and a TWA Constellation collide in empty air space over the Grand Canyon.

1956 American college instructor Charles Van Doren becomes involved in the *Twenty-One* quiz show scandal.

1961 CIA-trained Cuban refugees fail to overthrow dictator Fidel Castro during the Bay of Pigs invasion.

1961 The U.S. Air Force begins spraying the defoliant Agent Orange in Vietnam.

1969 General Motors discontinues production of the controversial Chevrolet Corvair, America's first rear-engine automobile.

1970 American astronauts abort the *Apollo 13* mission to the Moon.

1972 A failed burglary at the offices of the Democratic National Committee sets the stage for the Watergate scandal.

1973 The United States ends its long and disastrous military involvement in the Vietnam War.

1939–45
World War II

1950
Korean War
begins

1962
Cuban missile
crisis

1965–73
The Vietnam
War

1940   1950   1960   1970

1978 The Ford Motor Company recalls 1.4 million Pinto automobiles after several fatal rear-impact collisions.

1979 The Three Mile Island nuclear power plant in Pennsylvania has an accidental meltdown.

1980 Love Canal, New York, is evacuated after years of toxic waste dumping make this residential area uninhabitable.

1980 Fire protection systems fail to prevent a blaze from engulfing the MGM Grand Hotel in Las Vegas, Nevada.

1980 U.S. military forces stage an aborted rescue of American hostages in Tehran, Iran.

1983 Artificial heart recipient Barney Clark dies 112 days after his historic surgery.

1983 The infamous copper mining "Pit" in Butte, Montana is closed.

1984 A poisonous gas cloud escapes from the Union Carbide chemical plant in Bhopal, India, killing thousands of people.

1986 Two mammoth explosions blow apart Unit 4 of the Chernobyl nuclear power plant in the Ukraine.

1986 The entire flight crew dies when the space shuttle *Challenger* explodes after launch.

1989 The oil tanker Exxon *Valdez* runs aground in Alaska, spilling 10.8 million gallons of crude oil and polluting 1,500 miles of shoreline.

1991 U.S. diplomatic failures help trigger the Persian Gulf War.

1992 Silicone breast implants are banned by the Food and Drug Administration.

1992 John Gotti, the "Teflon Don," is sentenced to life in prison after his underboss, Sammy "the Bull" Gravano, testifies against the Gambino crime family.

1974
President Richard M.
Nixon resigns

1983
The United States
invades Grenada

1989
The Berlin
Wall is
destroyed

1975   1980   1985

1992 American adventurer Christopher McCandless starves to death during an Alaskan wilderness trek.

1993 The U.S. Congress ends funding for the Superconductor Super Collider.

1994 U.S. figure skater Tanya Harding is implicated in an assault on fellow skater Nancy Kerrigan.

1994 CIA agent Aldrich Ames is convicted of spying for the Soviet Union.

1995 Twelve people die and thousands are injured in a nerve gas attack in Tokyo, Japan.

1995 English stock trader Nicholas Leeson triggers the collapse of Barings PLC.

1995 The controversial Denver International Airport in Colorado finally opens for business.

1996 The British government orders the slaughter of thousands of cattle infected with mad cow disease.

1996 Seven-year-old American pilot Jessica Dubroff dies while trying to set an aviation record.

1996 Seven climbers perish during a blizzard on Mount Everest.

1997 The MRTA hostage crisis at the Japanese embassy in Lima, Peru, reaches a violent climax.

1997 The Canadian Bre-X mining company is shut down after the world's largest "gold discovery" proves to be a hoax.

1997 American scientist Karen Wetterhahn dies after being exposed to liquid mercury during a laboratory experiment.

1998 Federal Aviation Administration technicians conclude that the mainframe computer used in the nation's largest air traffic control centers is "Year 2000" compliant.

1992
Los Angeles
riots

1995
Yitzhak Rabin
is assassinated

1998
President
Bill Clinton
visits China

1990   1995   2000

Great Misadventures

Erik the Red and Norse Settlement in Greenland

986 TO C. 1500

T he discovery of Greenland came about as the result of a bitter quarrel. Norse explorer Erik the Red found and settled the country in 986 after being banished from Iceland because he had killed two men in a blood feud. (A blood feud is a conflict between two kinship groups over a wrong done to a relative.) After establishing the Norse Greenland community according to Viking traditions, Erik was distressed when his son Leif Erikkson (born c. 1000) brought Christianity back from Norway. The Norse prospered in Greenland for several hundred years, but changing climatic patterns gradually made the country too cold for European farming practices. These harsh conditions eventually led to the extinction of the Norsemen in Greenland by the early sixteenth century.

Harsh conditions eventually led to the extinction of the Norse settlement in Greenland by the early sixteenth century.

Erik discovers Greenland

When Erik was banished from Iceland, he decided to go in search of "Ulffson's Land." Erik had often heard about the voyages of Norwegian explorer Gunnbjörn Ulffson. In his travels, Ulffson had discovered a group of small islands west of Iceland. Ulffson claimed to have seen a much larger island beyond this smaller group. This landmass later became known as "Ulffson's Land." Gathering together a group of retainers (or employees)

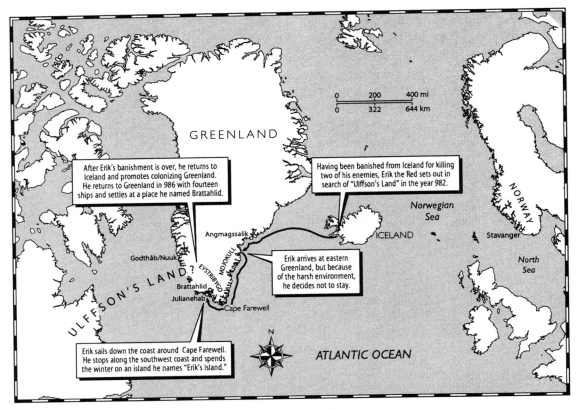

Within the map:

GREENLAND

NORWAY

Norwegian Sea

ICELAND

Stavanger

North Sea

After Erik's banishment is over, he returns to Iceland and promotes colonizing Greenland. He returns to Greenland in 986 with fourteen ships and settles at a place he named Brattahlid.

Having been banished from Iceland for killing two of his enemies, Erik the Red sets out in search of "Ulffson's Land" in the year 982.

Angmagssalik

MDJOKULL

Godthåb/Nuuk

EYSTRIBYGO

ULFFSON'S LAND?

Brattahlid

Julianehåb

Cape Farewell

Erik arrives at eastern Greenland, but because of the harsh environment, he decides not to stay.

Erik sails down the coast around Cape Farewell. He stops along the southwest coast and spends the winter on an island he names "Erik's Island."

N

ATLANTIC OCEAN

0 200 400 mi
0 322 644 km

Erik the Red's travels to and from Greenland, beginning in 982.

in the year 982, Erik set out for Ulffson's Land by sailing due west from a peninsula called Snaefellsnes. He soon sighted Gunnbjorn's Skerries, thought to be off Cape Dan in eastern Greenland near the modern town of Angmagssalik. Erik eventually touched land on the shore of eastern Greenland at a place named Mdjokull ("Middle Glacier"). Due to the flow of air currents, eastern Greenland has a much harsher environment and is more barren (lacking in plant and animal life) and icebound than western Greenland. Because of these severe conditions, Erik did not stay long at Mdjokull.

Searching for a more favorable location, Erik sailed south down the coast and rounded the southern tip at present-day Cape Farewell. He then stopped along the southwest coast at an area later known as the "Eastern Settlement." Erik spent the winter on an island he named "Erik's Island." In the spring of 983 he sailed up the nearby fjord (a narrow inlet of the sea between cliffs or steep slopes of ice) that he also named after himself. After spending the next winter on the southern tip of Greenland, Erik and his party sailed up the east coast in the spring of 984. He returned to spend the following winter on Erik's Island.

Settles Greenland

By this time Erik's banishment was over, so he was able to return to Iceland. He sailed around the southern tip of Greenland and returned safely to Breidafjord in Iceland in the summer of 985. Upon Erik's return, however, the blood feud with his neighbors was revived. As a result, Erik began to promote colonization (the establishment of settlements) in Greenland. In 986 he left Iceland with fourteen ships that carried between four and five hundred people, as well as domestic animals and household goods. Erik's group settled at a place he named Brattahlid (now a trading station called Qagssiarssuk) at the head of Erik's Fjord, which became the center of the Eastern Settlement. The Western Settlement (near present-day Nuuk) was about 180 miles farther up the coast. Many smaller settlements lay in between the two sites.

Farms built with stone and peat (rotted vegetable matter) multiplied as new colonists arrived from Norway and Iceland. In summer, there was deep green grass for cattle, and the settlers hunted hares (mammals similar to rabbits), reindeer, and foxes. It was not long before the Norsemen began to trade with the "Skraelings," or Eskimos, exchanging corn and iron from Norway for walrus ivory and the skins of bears and

EIREKUR hinn Raude, Syrste Landnams mann Granlands.

Hop byga a Granlande. MXXIO 986.

Norse explorer Erik the Red found and settled Greenland after being banished from Iceland due to a blood feud.

seals. (Eskimos are a group of peoples living in the Arctic coastal regions of North America, parts of Greenland, and northeast Siberia.)

Christianity comes to Greenland

In the year 999, Erik's son Leif pioneered the first direct route to Norway from Greenland. While in Norway, Leif converted to Christianity and brought back the first missionary with him to Greenland. This did not please Erik, who remained true to the old Viking religion. When Erik's son Thorsteinn the Unlucky decided to make a trip to Vinland sometime between 1001 and 1005, Erik wanted to go with him. (Vinland was a section of North America discovered by Leif in the eleventh century. No one has been able to determine exactly where Vinland was located, although areas from Newfoundland to Virginia have been suggested as likely places by historical researchers.) Erik fell off his horse on the way to the ship, however, and injured his leg. He died sometime during the winter of 1003–04 (ironically, on the grounds of what became the Christian cathedral at Brattahlid).

Climate shifts take toll

The Norse Greenland settlements prospered for a while. The various communities were even declared a crown (royal) colony of Norway in 1261. As the years passed, however, the settlements fell upon hard times. The milder climate that had allowed for European farming practices turned colder, and the build-up of ice in the ocean made communication with Iceland increasingly more difficult. Deprived of resources from their mother country, Norse farmers in Greenland were excused payment of their tithes (payments) to the Catholic Church in 1345.

Around 1350 the Inuit advancing from the north are thought to have overwhelmed the Western Settlement. (The term "Inuit" refers to the Eskimo peoples of North America, especially Arctic Canada and Greenland.) Rumors began to spread that, in their desperation, the Norse had cast off Christianity for the pagan (non-Christian) religion of the Eskimos. For a brief time, missionaries were sent to Greenland in hope of saving the settlers; unfortunately, few people could withstand the journey to and from Iceland through the rough and frigid seas. The last recorded voyage between Iceland and Greenland was made in 1410 (although later trips may have been made). A letter written by Pope Alexander VI in 1492 stated that the Norse settlers were living a miserable existence on dried fish and milk. No ship from Norway or Iceland had reached the island in eighty years.

Death of the Norse settlements

A few survivors of the Norse settlements may have lived until the early sixteenth century. Excavations (archaeological digs) made in the Norse cemetery of Herjolfness in South Greenland, however, revealed the suffering the settlers had endured. Their bodies, which had been mummified (preserved) by the ice, were very thin, diseased, and in some cases, deformed by intermarriage. Underneath the bodies' wooden coffins were the tree roots and plants Erik had seen when he arrived in the time of a warmer, more favorable climate. By the time British arctic explorer Sir Martin Frobisher saw the coast of Greenland in 1576, the Viking population had disappeared.

FOR FURTHER REFERENCE

Books

Byers, Paula K., and Suzanne M. Bourgoin, eds. *Encyclopedia of World Biography*. 2nd ed. Detroit: Gale, 1998, pp. 304–05.

Marcus, G. J. *The Conquest of the North Atlantic*. New York City: Oxford University Press, 1981.

The Children's Crusade

1212

The Children's Crusade was a religious march that took place in Europe during the summer of 1212. Stephen of Cloyes, a shepherd boy, visited King Philip Augustus of France and said that Jesus, disguised as a poor pilgrim, had handed him a letter for the king. (Jesus of Nazareth was the founder of Christianity.) In the letter Jesus urged Philip to send Stephen on a crusade to the Holy Land. (Now known as Palestine, the Holy Land is a region comprised of parts of present-day Israel, Jordan, and Egypt. The area is considered sacred by Jews, Muslims, and Christians.) When Philip was not moved by Stephen's petition, the boy began to tour the countryside, encouraging other children to join him. After seeing the depth of Stephen's following, Philip officially organized the Children's Crusade. The group, however, never reached the Holy Land. Instead, the Crusade ended tragically when most of the children were sold off as slaves.

The Children's Crusade ended tragically when most of the young crusaders were sold as slaves.

The Crusades

The Children's Crusade was never a crusade in the official sense of the term because it was not approved of or blessed by the pope (the head of the Roman Catholic Church). Stephen's marchers never received the dispensations (forgiveness of sin), holy relics (holy objects), and legal protections given to men who had "taken the cross" (committed themselves to a Christian mission). Unlike the nine Crusades involving adult "Christian soldiers," the child crusaders never left Western Europe. Some historians now view the trek as an outbreak of mass hysteria disguised as religious behavior.

The Crusades were a series of holy wars launched by Pope Urban II (c. 1035–1099) in 1095. The original goal of the Crusades was to recapture the Holy Land. Crusaders especially wanted to regain the Holy City of Jerusalem, which was held by the "Saracens" (Muslims; followers of the Islamic religion). Many crusaders, however, were more interested in raiding and robbing than in fulfilling a religious mission. In 1204, for example, soldiers in the Fourth Crusade spent most of their time attacking other Christians. This particular crusade ended in the ransacking (or raiding) of the predominantly Christian city of Constantinople (present-day Istanbul, Turkey).

Crusaders were often members of the surplus population of Europe, which by the twelfth and thirteenth centuries was greater than the land could easily support. Many crusaders followed crusade-preachers across Europe in the name of rescuing the Holy Land. But thousands of crusaders actually wanted to start a new life in the East, and for a time they were able to sustain crusader kingdoms in the Holy Land. The last crusader stronghold, at Acre, fell to the Muslims in 1291.

Stephen delivers letter to Philip

In May 1212 the king of France, Philip Augustus (1165–1223), was visited in his court at Saint Denis by Stephen, a twelve-year-old shepherd boy from the town of Cloyes near Orléans. Stephen arrived in the company of other local shepherds and told the king that Jesus, disguised as a poor pilgrim, had miraculously visited him while he was watching his sheep. Stephen offered bread to this pilgrim who, in return, handed him a letter for the king, urging the boy to go on a crusade. The king was not impressed by this story, but Stephen soon showed that he had great abilities as a preacher. He began to tour the countryside, persuading other children to join him.

According to legend, Stephen soon raised a force of 30,000 children, ages twelve and under, who he instructed to rally at the town of Vendome before setting out on the journey to the

Holy Land. Pope Innocent III (1160 or 1161–1216), an ardent advocate of crusading, is supposed to have said, "These children put us to shame, because while we sleep they rush to recover the Holy Land."

As early historians tell it, the majority of children—both boys and girls—began their walk by moving toward the southern French coast. Stephen was given a decorated cart with a sun shade. He was regarded by many of the other children as a living saint whose hair and clothing threads had miraculous healing powers. The children's only food would have come from the communities through which the group passed. But people in these towns could not have managed to feed several thousand newcomers, however admiring they may have been of the children's courage. As a result, many child crusaders suffered from hunger and thirst.

Crusaders wait for sea to part

Arriving in Marseilles at last, those children who had not already dropped out of the march or starved to death camped in the streets. They then gathered at the waterfront on the Mediterranean Sea, preparing to see the waters part as they had for Moses during the escape of the Children of Israel from Egypt. (According to the Hebrew Bible, when the prophet Moses led the Israelites out of captivity in Egypt, the Red Sea parted so that they could walk back to the Holy Land.) Stephen had been told in a dream that the waters would part again so that his crusaders could also walk to the Holy Land, but the miracle did not take place. Many of the children denounced

Stephen as a false prophet, but others waited, expecting that God would soon fulfill his promise and enable them to march across the water to Jerusalem.

Crusade takes disastrous turn

Meanwhile, two local merchants named Iron Hugo and William the Pig offered to pay for ships to take the children on the next stage of their journey. Stephen accepted the offer, and the children boarded seven vessels. Due to the treachery of these two merchants, however, the children were headed for the slave markets of North Africa rather than the Holy Land. Two of the ships broke up in a storm and sank, drowning everyone on board. The other five ships were soon in enemy hands at Bougie, Algeria. Most of the children were then sold into slavery, and for nearly two decades no further word was heard of them. Pope Gregory IX (1170–1241) later built the Church of the New Innocents on the island of Recluse, where the two ships were lost. The bodies of the children who had been washed ashore were preserved at the church.

Stephen never heard from again

Eighteen years later, a priest appeared in France with the news that he—one of the few adults to accompany the Children's Crusade—had been enslaved like the children. The priest had enjoyed a tolerable captivity at the hands of a scholarly caliph (an Islamic religious leader) who had learned about Western ways from the captive and his fellow priests. The priest also reported, however, that another 700 captives had been tortured into becoming Muslims. The captives were sent to work on plantations in Egypt belonging to the governor of Alexandria. The priest said that eighteen more captives had been taken to Baghdad (the capital of present-day Iraq), where they had been slain after refusing to recant (renounce) their Christian faith. Nothing was known, however, about Stephen's fate.

◀ The Children's Crusade was a religious march that took place in Europe during the summer of 1212. The march—which included thousands of young boys and girls—was organized by a shepherd boy named Stephen of Cloyes.

The Children's Crusade was not the last episode of its kind. In 1237 more than 1,000 children were seized by what appears to have been a form of St. Vitus's Dance (a disease that causes violent twitching in the body). The children are said to have made their way from Erfurt to Amstadt in Germany. In 1251 a group of shepherds, like Stephen of Cloyes, also claimed to have a letter from Jesus. The shepherds then set out to rescue their captive king, Louis IX (1214–1270), from the Holy Land. Perhaps the most famous incident of all reportedly took place in June 1284. A handsome young man with a silver flute is said to have appeared in the German city of Hamlin and with his music spirited away 130 boys who were never seen again. The "Pied Piper of Hamlin" story is often compared with the tale of the Children's Crusade, which occurred seventy years earlier.

Second Children's Crusade formed

The French Children's Crusade was imitated by a group of German children who had a "Stephen of Cloyes" of their own, a boy named Nicholas. Like Stephen, Nicholas was a preacher. His following of boys and girls came from the Rhine valley. Nicholas's ever-growing band of children marched south across the Alps to Genoa, a city on the Italian coast. According to some historians, the German children—like their French counterparts—declared their intent to walk across the sea on dry land and recover Jerusalem and the Holy Land. Another version of the story says that the children believed they could walk on the tops of the waves without getting their feet wet.

Another tragic ending

As with the young French crusaders, the sea did not part for the German travelers. The group began to break up, with some children going to Venice and Brindisi in Italy, and some back to Marseilles, France. Many other youngsters boarded ships that went not to the Holy Land, but to a life of slavery. A few children, including Nicholas, journeyed to Rome to see Pope Innocent III. Innocent told the children to go back to their homes. Nicholas went on to fight in battles of the later Crusades and is reported to have returned to Germany unharmed.

FOR FURTHER REFERENCE

Books

Rhodes, Evan H. *An Army of Children: The Story of the Children's Crusade, 1212.* New York: Dial Press, 1978.

Setton, Kenneth, ed. "The Children's Crusade," by Norman Zacour in *A History of the Crusades.* Madison: University of Wisconsin Press, 1969, pp. 325–42.

Christopher Columbus in Hispaniola

1498

Christopher Columbus left Hispaniola for Spain in chains and under arrest, his career and his reputation permanently damaged.

Christopher Columbus was an Italian explorer who made four voyages to the Caribbean and South America between 1492 and 1504. As governor of Hispaniola, Columbus oversaw the establishment of the first European settlements in the Americas. The first European to see the continent of South America, Columbus brought other Europeans to the Americas, with devastating consequences to the native people the explorer called "Indians." The mistreatment of these people by the Spanish colonists was so cruel that it became known in Europe as "The Black Legend," a terrible story of tyranny (the abuse of power) and exploitation (the use of one person by another for selfish purposes).

Beginning with Columbus's rule as governor, the natives of Hispaniola entered a period of decline that eventually left them virtually exterminated. Columbus was and is a figure of controversy. On the one hand, he accomplished a great deal for Spain. On the other, he left Hispaniola for Spain in chains and under arrest, his career and reputation permanently damaged. Even today, historians cannot agree on whether Columbus was a great visionary, or a self-absorbed and incompetent man whose success was due mostly to lucky accidents.

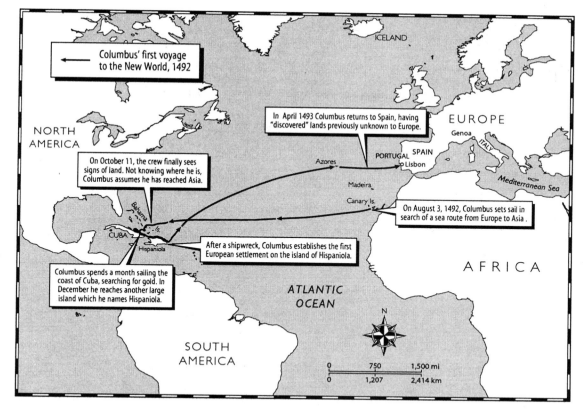

On August 3, 1492, Christopher Columbus set sail from the Canary Islands in search of a sea route from Europe to Asia.

A daring idea

In the early 1480s ship captain Christopher Columbus began to seek a sponsor (a financial backer) for a voyage of exploration. He wanted to prove his theory about a sea route from Europe to Asia, which the Europeans were eager to find. Columbus believed it would be faster and easier to get to Asia by sailing west across the Atlantic Ocean than by sailing around Africa and into the Indian Ocean, as the Portuguese were then trying to do.

Educated Europeans of the fifteenth century knew that the earth was a sphere. In theory, Columbus's idea would work, but no one knew how large the globe was. Columbus, for example, believed the Earth was much smaller than it actually is. He claimed that the distance from Portugal to Japan would prove to be about 2,400 nautical miles, while it is actually more than ten thousand. (A nautical mile is a unit of distance used in navigation, equal to approximately 6,080 feet, or slightly longer than the measure of a mile on land.)

For several years Columbus tried to sell his idea to the king of Portugal. He did not succeed for two reasons. First, the king's advisers believed that Columbus's estimates of the distances were much too small. In addition, a Portuguese navigator named Bartolomeu Dias (c. 1450–1500) had successfully sailed around the southern tip of Africa in 1488. This meant a sea passage from Europe to India had already been found. The Portuguese were no longer interested in Columbus's ideas.

Help from the Spanish queen

Not to be discouraged, Columbus went to try his luck in Spain. He first met with Queen Isabella (1451–1504) in 1486. Her advisers also believed Columbus was wrong about the size of the world, but after some discussion they concluded that he should be allowed to make his attempt. Columbus wanted to make sure that his theory, if correct, would pay off not only for Spain, but for himself. He negotiated a financial reward for his discoveries, as well as titles and the right to govern any lands he discovered.

In April 1492 Queen Isabella and King Ferdinand (1452–1516) signed an agreement with Columbus called "The Capitulations," in which the monarchs agreed to finance the explorer's voyage of exploration. In addition, Columbus would be named admiral, become the governor of any lands he discovered, and receive—tax-free—ten percent of any riches found in the new lands. These rights could later be passed on to Columbus's heirs. On August 3, 1492, three ships—the *Santa Maria* (with Columbus as captain), the *Niña,* and the *Pinta*—set sail on an historic journey.

Queen Isabella of Spain provided financial support for Christopher Columbus's search for a sea route to Asia.

First lands in Bahamas

The ships made good progress across the Atlantic, but as the weeks passed, the crew became nervous. By September 19, if Columbus's theory was right, they should have been in sight of land, but they were not. The ship traveled hundreds of miles farther. On October 10 the crew began to turn mutinous (angry and threatening the captain's authority), wanting to go back. The next day, however, the sailors saw signs of land: branches with green leaves and flowers floating in the water. Early the following morning a lookout on the *Pinta* sighted white cliffs in the moonlight and shouted, "Tierra! Tierra!" ("Land! Land!").

The land the group had found was a small island in the present-day Bahamas (a group of islands southeast of Florida). Not knowing where he was, Columbus assumed he had reached Asia, or the "Indies." He therefore called the native people he met on the island "Indians." When the native people told Columbus about a larger island to the south, he thought it must be part of China or Japan. Actually the landmass was the island now called Cuba.

The lure of gold

Columbus spent a month sailing along the coast of Cuba, looking for gold. In early December 1492 he reached another large island, which he named Hispaniola because it reminded him so much of Spain ("Espanola" means "Spanish". This was the island that today is comprised of the countries of Haiti and the Dominican Republic.) Sailing eastward along the north coast of Hispaniola, Columbus finally found what he was looking for. He met a young chief who was wearing gold ornaments that he gladly traded for European goods. Farther east, Columbus met a more important chief who had even larger gold pieces.

Shipwreck decides location of first settlement

An accident led Columbus to establish the first European settlement of the Americas on Hispaniola. The chief with the large gold ornaments and his people were aboard the *Santa Maria* on Christmas Eve as Columbus's guests. When the celebration was over, everyone fell asleep and the *Santa Maria* hit a coral reef. The ship was damaged beyond repair. With the help of the local tribe, the Spanish were able to unload most of the goods from the ship and carry them to shore.

Making the best of a bad situation, Columbus founded the first European settlement in the Americas on that site, a small bay where the Haitian village of Limonade-Bord-de-Mer now stands. He named the settlement La Navidad ("The Birth") in honor of the fact that the colony was founded on Christmas Day. When Columbus left La Navidad a few weeks later to return to Spain, twenty-one men remained in the settlement under the command of Diego de Harana, the cousin of Columbus's mistress. Thus began the Spanish colonization of the Americas.

Columbus returned to Spain, having discovered lands previously unknown to Europe. Since he also brought evidence of gold and other possible riches, he had no trouble winning support for a second voyage. The Spanish crown outfitted him with seventeen ships. Well over one thousand colonists sailed with Columbus on this second journey. When the expedition reached La Navidad in November 1493, however, the settlement lay in ruins. Unburied Spanish bodies were everywhere. Either the demands of the Spanish on the Indians had turned the natives against the Europeans, leading to war, or the Spaniards had fought among themselves. No one had survived to tell the story.

A new settlement at Isabela

Abandoning the site, Columbus took his new colonists seventy-five miles east to a small, shallow bay where he built a settlement called Isabela. Isabela was constructed in the Spanish style, with a church and a government building located on a central square. There were two hundred huts for the settlers.

The admiral wasted no time in pursuing the gold that would enrich Spain and secure his position and power. Only four days after landing at Isabela, Columbus sent Alonso de Ojeda (1465–1515), an officer, to look for gold. Ojeda found a little gold in the mountains of the interior. It would be several years, however, before a major gold strike was made.

While Ojeda was looking for gold, Columbus set off to explore nearby islands. A curious incident occurred during this time. At one point Columbus gathered all his men together and made them swear to an oath that the coast they had been sailing along (that of Cuba) was not the coast of an island, but was part of the mainland of Asia. Columbus was still convinced—or was trying to convince himself—that he had found the Indies. If he suspected he had made a geographical mistake, he apparently did not want news of it to come from his men.

Outrages against the native people

Columbus returned to Isabela in late September 1494. There he found tensions growing between the native tribes and the Spaniards, whom he had ordered "to patrol the country and reduce it to the service of the Catholic Sovereigns." The colonists were mistreating the natives by taking them as slaves, stealing from them, and raping and beating them at will. As Columbus's son Fernando later wrote, "The Admiral found the island in a pitiful state, with most of the Christians committing innumerable outrages for which they were mortally hated by the Indians, who refused to obey them."

Christopher Columbus made a poor governor of Hispaniola. In fact, by 1498 Spanish colonists on the island were openly challenging Columbus's leadership abilities.

The native people of Hispaniola soon realized that the arrival of the Spanish meant their destruction. They began organizing an army to try and drive the Europeans off the island. The Spanish took harsh steps to subdue these plans. In March 1495 Columbus and his brother Bartholomeo (c. 1445–c. 1514) led an attack on the tribes. The Spanish had 220 soldiers in full armor—some mounted on horses, with all types of European weaponry—and 20 dogs. This force completely defeated the natives. During the next few years the people of Hispaniola were rapidly driven toward extinction.

Slavery, forced labor, extreme punishment

The government the Spaniards established in Hispaniola was harsh. Columbus instituted a tribute system, which required a certain amount of gold be gathered by every native person over the age of fourteen. This measure of gold had to be delivered to the Spanish every three months. People who did not pay the tribute were punished severely (for example, their hands were cut off). Another formal government policy was forced labor. Colonists were assigned native people to use as they liked for a variety of difficult tasks.

Native offenses against the Spanish were punished with hanging, burning at the stake, beheading, or amputation. Meanwhile, the Spaniards on the island acted without restraint, often attacking or killing men, women, and children on a whim. Other native people were taken to Spain to be sold as slaves—thirty by Columbus himself, and later three hundred by his brother Bartholomeo.

A people destroyed

The native people of Hispaniola also died because of the diseases the Europeans brought with them. The island's native population had no previous contact with illnesses such as smallpox (a highly infectious viral disease), and no resistance to them. Meanwhile, the first unfavorable reports about conditions in Hispaniola were beginning to reach King Ferdinand and Queen Isabella.

There was little gold returning to Spain, the colonists had many complaints, and almost no natives had been converted to

Catholicism. Columbus was obliged to return to Spain in 1496 to try to explain the situation to the monarchy. Apparently the king and queen had lost most of their confidence in Columbus's ability to govern the colony. It was some time before he could convince the rulers to send him back to Hispaniola. During the two years he spent trying to restore the monarchs' faith in him, Columbus wore the coarse dress of a Franciscan friar (a member of the Roman Catholic monastic order). The explorer's strange attire has never been well understood, but he may have adopted it out of regret for wrongdoing, to show humility, or even as a disguise.

Columbus returns to Hispaniola

Finally the king and queen gave Columbus command of a small fleet carrying supplies to Hispaniola. He set sail in May 1498. During this third voyage he sailed to the coast of Venezuela, becoming the first European to see the continent of South America. Columbus had left his brother Bartholomeo in command at Isabela. In order to get a better site for the Spanish headquarters, Bartholomeo moved the settlement to the south side of the island to a place the Spanish named Santo Domingo. Columbus reached Santo Domingo in August 1498. He settled down in a large stone house and for the next two years tried to govern the island. He was not up to the job, however, and more trouble began.

The colonists rebel

The Spanish colonists had many complaints. Until the big gold strike of late 1499, the gold that could be found was in small quantities and required a great deal of labor to extract. Because so many of the native people had either run away or died, the Spaniards could not get enough workers. There was constant friction between the remaining native inhabitants and the colonists. Death and sickness were everywhere, and large number of colonists were sick at any given time with deadly diseases. Supplies were also scarce and living conditions poor. Life on Hispaniola was not what the settlers had been led to believe. By 1498 the colonists were openly challenging the authority of Columbus.

CHRISTOPHER COLUMBUS

Christopher Columbus was born in the city of Genoa, Italy, in 1451. His family, who made and traded woolen fabrics, had lived in Genoa for at least three generations. As a young man, Columbus worked as a sailor on merchant and war ships in the Mediterranean Sea. He went to Lisbon, Portugal, in 1476, to learn mathematics and astronomy (subjects that were vital for navigation). In 1478 Columbus got married and settled on Madeira (an island off the northwest coast of Africa), where his son Diego was born. He had another son, Fernando, with his Spanish mistress, Beatriz Enriquez, in 1488. In 1492 Queen Isabella of Spain agreed to sponsor Columbus's first voyage of exploration. Columbus spent the following eight years exploring and administering lands he encountered in the "New World" (the term the Europeans used to describe the Americas). He was a failure as a governor, however, and eventually left Hispaniola as a prisoner. His career never recovered, and Columbus died in 1506 a wealthy but disappointed man.

Columbus made a very poor governor. It appears he was more interested in managing his own fortune and promoting himself to the Spanish crown than in solving the problems of the colonists. In a letter to the king and queen he even complained that he wanted "to escape from governing a dissolute [immoral] people [the Spanish] who fear neither God nor their king and queen, being full of folly and malice." He seems to have had little talent for leadership, going from severely repressive measures to neglect and back again. Columbus did not have the respect of the Spaniards, and he could not maintain order.

Bobadilla arrests Columbus

The Spanish king and queen continued to hear criticism about the administration of Hispaniola by the Columbus brothers. For this reason they sent a trusted knight, Francisco de Bobadilla (died 1502), to replace Columbus as the new governor. When Bobadilla arrived in Santo Domingo in August 1500, he found the Spanish colony in chaos. The bodies of seven rebel Spaniards were hanging in the town square, and Columbus's brother Diego was planning to hang five more the following day. Columbus himself was not in Santo Domingo because he had gone to try to subdue a rebellion in another part of the island. His brother Bartholomeo was doing the same elsewhere. Bobadilla immediately put Diego in jail, then arrested the other brothers as soon as they were found.

The admiral's "great dishonor"

The colonists made many serious accusations against Columbus and his brothers. After a hearing, Bobadilla decided to send the men back to Spain for trial. In chains, the three brothers walked to the ships that would take them to Europe. Crowds of angry colonists shouted insults at them as they passed. It was a painful moment for the former governor. He later described his "great dishonor" to the king and queen as follows: "Suddenly, when I was expecting the arrival of ships to take me to your royal presence, bearing triumph and great tidings of gold, in great joy and security, I was arrested and cast into a ship with my two brothers, shackled with chains and naked in body, and treated very badly, without being brought to trial or convicted."

After months as a prisoner, Columbus was summoned to see Ferdinand and Isabella. He tried to convince them of his innocence and asked for the restoration of all his titles, including governor. The king and queen permitted him to keep his title of admiral, but they appointed a new governor, Nicolas de Ovando (c. 1451–c. 1511), for Hispaniola.

Final voyage a disaster

In 1502 Columbus set out on one more voyage of exploration to the Caribbean. This final trip was beset with misfortune and humiliation, however, and did nothing to improve his position. In fact, Columbus actually had to be rescued after spending a year marooned in Jamaica. Eventually he made his way back to Spain. Although he was ill, Columbus had plenty of money from his share of the gold from Hispaniola. He asked to be sent to sea again, but King Ferdinand refused. Columbus retired to a house in Valladolid, Spain, and died in 1506.

FOR FURTHER REFERENCE
Books

Sale, Kirkpatrick. *The Conquest of Paradise: Christopher Columbus and the Columbian Legacy.* New York City: Knopf, 1990.

Pedro de Alvarado's Trek to Quito

1532 TO 1534

When Alvarado's expedition reached the Incan highway, the group discovered that another conquistador had already claimed Quito and the surrounding area for Spain.

During the sixteenth century Spanish expeditions swept through the New World (the term the Europeans used to describe the Americas), conquering Aztec, Incan, and Mayan empires in Mexico and Central America. The Spanish military leaders, who were called conquistadors, were notorious for their greediness and their brutality as they competed with one another to seize wealth and power. Among the most ruthless conquistadors was Pedro de Alvarado. Fueled by grand visions of conquering Quito, a rich Incan city in Ecuador, Alvarado set out on an unauthorized expedition from Guatemala across the Andes mountains in 1533. Traveling with Alvarado were five hundred Spanish soldiers and four thousand Guatemalans he had taken as slaves. When Alvarado's party reached the Incan highway six months later, the group discovered that another conquistador had already claimed Quito and the surrounding area for Spain. By this time Alvarado's misadventure had turned into a true tragedy. Eighty-five soldiers and at least two thousand slaves had lost their lives during the futile trip through the cold climate of the Andes.

Career plagued by disaster

Alvarado's career was plagued by disasters that resulted from his poor judgment and impetuous behavior. He em-

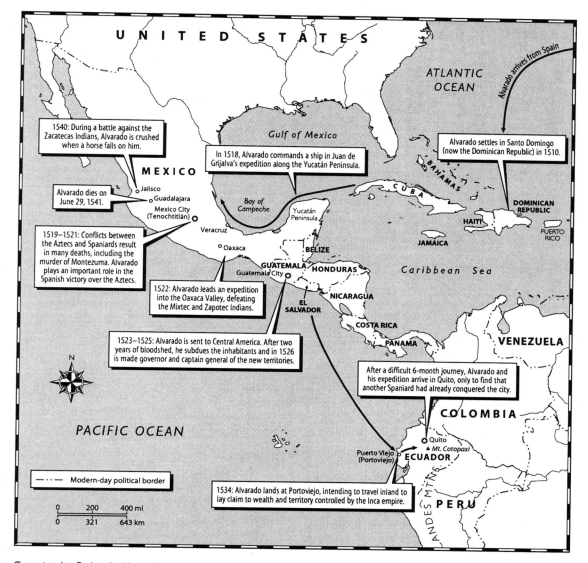

Conquistador Pedro de Alvarado spent many years subduing the native tribes of Mexico and Central America.

barked on his first major venture as a conquistador in February 1519. The Spanish governor of the New World, Diego Velásquez (1465–1524), appointed Alvarado chief lieutenant to the conquistador Hernán Cortés (1485–1547) on an expedition to conquer the Aztecs in Mexico. The Spanish forces entered the Aztec capital of Tenochtitlán (on the site of present-day Mexico City) the following November. From the outset

Cortés and Alvarado experienced a clash in cultures that not only revealed the Spaniards' ignorance of Aztec religion and customs, but also foreshadowed a disastrous series of events later caused by Alvarado.

Montezuma II thinks conquistadors are gods

Thinking that Cortés and Alvarado were descendants of the god Quetzalcoatl, the Aztec emperor Montezuma II (1466–1520) at first tried to persuade the men to leave by offering them expensive gifts. When the Spanish leaders refused the emperor's offer he apparently concluded they were indeed gods and that he must obey them. Montezuma II welcomed the Spanish into his palace, but Cortés soon decided they would be safer if they took the emperor hostage. Montezuma II was installed in Spanish quarters, where he was effectively held prisoner. While the Aztec ruler lived with the Europeans he gave them many gifts, including large amounts of gold.

In April 1520, Cortés and Alvarado took over an Aztec temple and turned it into a shrine to the Virgin Mary (the mother of Jesus of Nazareth, the founder of Christianity). Reporting that the angry Aztec gods had ordered Cortés killed in retaliation for this desecration, Montezuma II warned the conquistador to leave Tenochtitlán at once. In a rather mixed blessing, at that time Cortés also received word that a rival conquistador, Pánfilo de Narvaez, was headed toward the east coast of Mexico with orders from Velázquez to replace Cortés as the Spanish leader in the territory. Escaping the Aztec death edict, Cortés immediately departed with heavy forces in a campaign to defeat Narvaez.

Alvarado attacks Aztec nobles

In an agreement with Montezuma II, Alvarado was left in command of the remaining 140 Spanish soldiers in Tenochtitlán. Soon after the departure of Cortés, the Aztec rulers celebrated an important religious ceremony in the main square of the city. In response, Alvarado hastily blocked off the entrances to the square. The reasons for Alvarado's actions are unclear: He may have thought the ceremony was leading up to a massacre of his army, or he may have seen a unique opportunity to increase his control over the Aztecs. Whatever the reason, the small Spanish force then attacked the Aztecs, killing two hundred nobles. Set upon by an infuriated mob, Alvarado and his men were forced to retreat to the palace of Axayácatl, where they were further attacked.

Montezuma II is stoned to death

Cortés returned after defeating Narvaez at Veracruz (a Spanish settlement on the Gulf of Mexico). Now increased in number with many of Navraez's defeated troops, the Spanish army was led by Cortés and Alvarado back into Tenochtitlán. Cortés soon discovered the tense situation Alvarado had created, however, as angry Aztecs converged on the Spanish. In an attempt to calm the mob, Cortés forced Montezuma II to appear before his people. According to some reports, the horrified Europeans looked on as the Aztecs stoned their ruler to death. Cortés ordered an immediate retreat.

While acting as the chief lieutenant to conquistador Hernán Cortés, Pedro de Alvarado led a series of attacks on the Aztec people of Mexico.

With Alvarado in charge of the rear guard (troops who provide protection behind the main body of forces) and the Aztec army in full pursuit, the Spanish left the city during the early morning hours of July 1, 1520. The Spanish called the event *Noche Triste,* or the "Sorrowful Night." By the time they had reached Otumba (a town about a hundred miles northeast of present-day Mexico City) and finally managed to drive off their attackers, at least 450 Spanish soldiers lay dead. Alvarado gained renown among his comrades during the exit from Tenochtitlán when he leaped over a wide gap in the causeway (highway) that led out of the city across Lake Texcoco. Yet he had also set in motion the catastrophe that resulted in the murder of Montezuma II, the loss of Tenochtitlán, and the deaths of hundreds of his own men.

Alvarado redeems himself

Alvarado redeemed himself when the Spanish returned to Tenochtitlán in May 1521. He played a major role in the battles that finally culminated in a Spanish victory three months later. Following the defeat of the Aztecs, Alvarado's fortunes soared along with his ambition and brutality. In 1522 he defeated the Mixtecs and Zapotecs south of Mexico City, where he left a party of Spaniards to establish the town of Oaxaca. The following year Cortés sent Alvarado to conquer the former Mayan territory of Guatemala. For two years Alvarado fought several brutal and bloody campaigns with the native peoples. Eventually, after great loss of human life, he subdued the inhabitants of areas that are now the countries of Guatemala and El Salvador in Central America. Returning to Spain in 1526 to report on his exploits, Alvarado was made governor and captain general of the new Spanish territories in Guatemala.

Alvarado sets his sights on Quito

When Alvarado went back to Guatemala to take up his posts, however, he was much more interested in adventure and conquest than in performing his administrative duties. Launching an ambitious scheme, he built a fleet of boats for sailing across the Pacific to see if he could reach Asia. In 1532 Alvarado heard about the incredible victories the Spanish were winning in the rich Incan cities of Peru (in present-day South America). Virtually on impulse, Alvarado decided not to sail to

Asia. He set his sights instead on Quito, a city in north-central Ecuador (a country directly north of Peru), which was rumored to be one of the wealthiest Incan capitals.

Quito had not yet been taken by the Spanish, since it was located north of territories granted to conquistador Francisco Pizarro (c. 1475–1541) in 1529. In order to reach the Incan highway that led into Quito, however, Alvarado would have to make an difficult journey through the Andes mountains. (The Andes is a great mountain system stretching along the west coast of South America northward from Tierra del Fuego in Chile to Panama.) Reports later revealed that Alvarado was so caught up in dreams of wealth and glory that he failed to consider the hazards of traveling through the harsh Andes climate during sumer.

The expedition departs

Thus Alvarado embarked on the expedition that was to make him one of the most infamous Spanish conquistadors. Leaving Guatemala for Ecuador in late 1533, he seized additional ships on the Pacific coast of Nicaragua along the way. Alvarado landed at Portoviejo (also called Puerto Viejo) on the coast of Ecuador in February 1534. In a letter to Francisco de Barrioneuvo, a Spanish official, Alvarado confidently wrote that he had left La Posección, Nicaragua, on January 23. He reported that his party included twelve ships and five hundred soldiers, all of whom "were accustomed to warfare in these parts and expeditions into the interior." Also traveling with Alvarado were four thousand Guatemalan Indians, inhabitants of a tropical region, whom the conquistador had forced into slavery for the trip across the Andes.

Barrioneuvo already knew the Alvarado expedition was doomed. He had earlier written to King Charles of Spain (1500–1558) that the Guatemalan Indians would probably die because they would not be able to adjust to the cold climate of the mountains, and because "Peru is sterile in food supplies." Commenting on the fact that Alvarado had pressed virtually entire local tribes into service as porters (supply carriers), Barrioneuvo continued: "They say that Guatemala and Nicaragua have been depopulated."

Competition from other conquistadors

In the meantime, two other conquistadors were heading for Quito. Sebastián de Belalcázar (1495–1551), a captain in Pizarro's army, had heard about Alvarado's expedition to the city, so he quickly organized his own unauthorized party in an attempt to claim the riches before Alvarado. Belalcázar's superior, Spanish leader Diego de Almagro, then set out for Quito to reprimand Belalcázar for disobeying orders. Alvarado was entirely unaware of these developments. Although his own expedition had not been authorized by the Spanish crown, at that point Alvarado still considered the city fair game for conquest.

As Alvarado departed from Potoviejo, he did not take the inland route directly northeast across the Andes toward Quito. For some reason he decided to travel north into the Ecuadoran jungles. Hacking their way through the dense undergrowth, Alvarado's men were assaulted by swarms of insects. Soon the food supply was running low, and disease began taking its toll. To make matters worse, the soldiers' weapons and armor rusted in the intense humidity. Struggling with great difficulty toward the town of Tombela in north-central Ecuador, the party was caught in an eruption of Mount Cotopaxi, which covered everyone with volcanic ash.

Traveling over the Andes

After the party had rested in Tombela, Alvarado again chose the wrong approach to the Andes. This time he took a route through one of the highest passes in the mountains, between Mounts Chimborazo and Carihuarazo. Traveling over the Andes proved to be extremely difficult. As Barrioneuvo had predicted, at least two thousand Guatemalans froze to death in the heavy snow and intensely cold midwinter temperatures. Eighty-five Spaniards also died and the party lost most of their horses. Six months after leaving Portoviejo, Alvarado's depleted expedition finally stumbled onto the Inca highway that crossed the Andes. Upon seeing the tracks of the Belalcázar and Almagro parties in the snow, Alvarado was stunned to see that the Spanish had already entered Quito. In fact, Almagro had arrived to find that Belalcázar was not guilty of insubordination after all. Belalcázar had conquered the city in the name of Pizarro and Almagro.

A dejected Alvarado proceeded toward Quito only to discover that an Incan army was preparing to attack his forces. That confrontation was averted, however, when Almagro sent out eight scouts, who were captured by Alvarado's men. In response, Almagro threatened an attack. Now Alvarado found he had a new enemy: his fellow Spaniards. Alvarado's exhausted soldiers, anxious to get their reward for the grueling trip across the Andes, were ready to go against Almagro's men and take Quito. Yet Almagro had the advantage because he represented the occupying Spanish forces. As the two sides prepared for battle, a series of last-minute negotiations prevented a bloody showdown that would have left the Spanish vulnerable to an Incan counter-attack. In August 1534, Alvarado turned his ships and equipment over to Almagro, who paid him a hundred thousand gold pesos (Spanish dollars). Alvarado's men were placed under the command of Pizarro. Almagro also conducted an inquiry into the mistreatment of Guatemalan natives by Alvarado and his men during the march across the Andes. Almagro then sent a highly critical report to King Charles in Spain.

Alvarado joins Coronado expedition

In spite of his past behavior, Alvarado was allowed to return to his post in Guatemala in 1534. Two years later he was also given command of Honduras. Meanwhile, his men continued their brutal treatment of the native people while serving under Almagro in Chile. Alvarado had his final misadventure in 1540. He had just revived his plans to sail to Asia when the

Spanish viceroy (representative of the king) in Mexico persuaded him to join Francisco Vazquez de Coronado (see "Exploration and Adventure" entry). Coronado was searching for the fabled Seven Cities of Cibola, which were rumored to contain vast amounts of gold and other treasures, in what is now New Mexico.

During the expedition Alvarado met his final misadventure while helping to put down a revolt by the Zacatecas Indians in Jalisco. He led a cavalry attack on a Zacatecas stronghold on the top of a mountain. After being pushed back three times, the Spanish panicked and fled from the pursuing Zacatecas warriors. As Alvarado was running down the mountain he was crushed as a horse fell on him. Gravely injured, Alvarado was taken to the city of Guadalajara where he died.

FOR FURTHER REFERENCE

Books

Hemming, John. *The Conquest of the Incas*. New York City: Penguin Books, 1987.

Francisco de Coronado's Quest for Gold

1538 TO 1541

Francisco de Coronado was a Spanish explorer who was duped into believing that he could find fabulous cities filled with gold in the New World. In 1538, as governor of New Galicia (a province northwest of present-day Mexico City), Coronado sent out an expedition to find the "Seven Cities of Cibola" and claim their wealth for Spain. When his search party returned home empty-handed, Coronado convinced the Spanish viceroy to support another expedition. During his three-year-long search for Cibola's riches, Coronado explored parts of the Rio Grande river valley and Kansas, and became the first European to reach Palo Duro Canyon (near present-day Amarillo, Texas). During all his long-ranging travels, however, Coronado never found gold or the famous cities. He eventually returned home with nothing—the tales of Cibola's great wealth had been a lie.

During his long-ranging travels, Coronado never found any gold or the legendary "Seven Cities of Cibola."

Fray Marcos tells story of Cibola

As a young man, Coronado sailed to Mexico with Spanish explorer Antonio de Mendoza (c. 1490–1552). In 1538 Coronado became the governor of New Galicia. Soon after assuming his post, Coronado outfitted Estevanico (c. 1500–1539; a North African Moslem slave), and Fray Marcos de Niza, a Franciscan friar (a brother in a Roman Catholic reli-

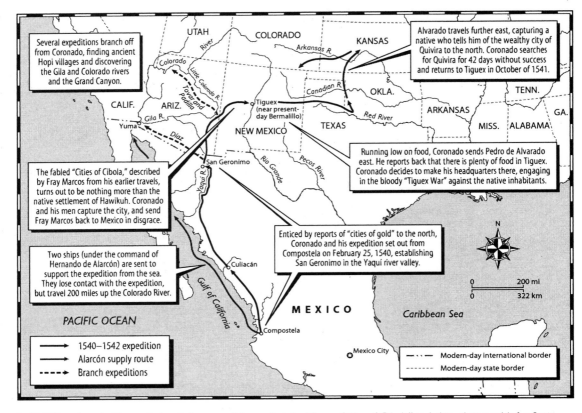

Several expeditions branch off from Coronado, finding ancient Hopi villages and discovering the Gila and Colorado rivers and the Grand Canyon.

Alvarado travels further east, capturing a native who tells him of the wealthy city of Quivira to the north. Coronado searches for Quivira for 42 days without success and returns to Tiguex in October of 1541.

Running low on food, Coronado sends Pedro de Alvarado east. He reports back that there is plenty of food in Tiguex. Coronado decides to make his headquarters there, engaging in the bloody "Tiguex War" against the native inhabitants.

The fabled "Cities of Cibola," described by Fray Marcos from his earlier travels, turns out to be nothing more than the native settlement of Hawikuh. Coronado and his men capture the city, and send Fray Marcos back to Mexico in disgrace.

Two ships (under the command of Hernando de Alarcón) are sent to support the expedition from the sea. They lose contact with the expedition, but travel 200 miles up the Colorado River.

Enticed by reports of "cities of gold" to the north, Coronado and his expedition set out from Compostela on February 25, 1540, establishing San Geronimo in the Yaquí river valley.

PACIFIC OCEAN

| 0 | 200 mi |
| 0 | 322 km |

MEXICO

Caribbean Sea

→ 1540–1542 expedition
→ Alarcón supply route
⇢ Branch expeditions

— · · · — Modern-day international border
— — — — Modern-day state border

In 1540 Francisco de Coronado headed an expedition to find the "Seven Cities of Cibola" and claim their wealth for Spain.

gious order), for an expedition. The two men were heading north to verify reports about the golden "Seven Cities of Cibola." The first stories about Cibola had originated with Estevanico, who had served as a guide on an expedition headed by Alvar Cabeza de Vaca (c. 1490–c. 1560). Fray Marcos's party left the town of Culiacán (the present-day capital of Sinaloa, a state in Mexico) on March 7, 1539.

Fray Marcos returned alone about five and a half months later. According to reports, Estevanico had been killed at the pueblo (native communal dwelling) of Hawikuh. Fray Marcos claimed that he had seen the large city of Cibola from a distance. (It is now believed that Fray Marcos was referring to Hawikuh, which was actually a small community.) Since his journal contained contradictory information about his travels, Fray Marcos added elaborate details to back up his story. These details impressed Coronado enough that the governor made plans to travel with Fray Marcos to Mexico City and bring back a report to Mendoza.

Coronado discovers Fray Marcos's deception

Mendoza liked Coronado's idea. He had long been interested in exploring the territory north of Mexico and was convinced by the friar's stories. Mendoza decided to equip an expedition at royal expense and named Coronado to head it. Coronado assembled a force of about 300 Spaniards and nearly 1,000 natives at the west coast town of Compostela. Mendoza traveled to Compostela to review the expedition in person before it started out on February 25, 1540. The viceroy also sent two ships up the Gulf of California under the command of Hernando de Alarcón to support the expedition from the sea. These ships lost contact with Coronado, but still managed to travel 200 miles up the Colorado River.

As governor of New Galicia, a province on the west coast of Mexico, Francisco de Coronado had jurisdiction over Spanish explorations on the northern frontier.

Coronado traveled with his army to Culiacán. On April 22 he left with an advance force of about one hundred Spaniards, a number of native people, and four friars. The group proceeded up the Yaqui River valley, where they founded the town of San Geronimo. Leaving one of his officers, Melchor Díaz, in charge, Coronado took a group of soldiers toward the Gila River. Díaz went up the Colorado near present-day Yuma, Arizona, and crossed into what is now California.

Coronado and his men had meanwhile crossed the Gila River and entered the Colorado Plateau. The group reached Hawikuh in what is now western New Mexico in early July. The Spanish had no difficulty capturing the town, but once inside they realized that it did not come close to matching Fray Marcos's glowing description. As a result, Coronado sent the friar back to Mexico in disgrace. One observer reported that "such were the curses that some hurled at Fray Marcos that I pray God may protect him from them."

ESTEVANICO'S MISADVENTURE

Estevanico was born in the town of Azemmour on the west coast of Morocco. Also known as "The Black" due to his probable African or part-African descent, he was captured and sold as a slave. Estevanico (which is a Spanish form of the name "Stephen") became the possession of a nobleman named Andres Dorantes de Carranca, whom he joined on an expedition to North America. After several misfortunes, Estevanico, Dorantes, and a man named Alonzo del Castillo Maldonado were captured by Native Americans at San Antonio Bay (on the coast of present-day Texas). The men eventually escaped and proceeded to travel the country as healers. Their reputation began to precede them, and they were welcome wherever they went. Along the way, Estevanico picked up a gourd from an Indian tribe and began to use it in his healing act. He was treated like a god among the Indians.

The four men reached Mexico City on July 24, 1536. They were well received by Viceroy Antonio Mendoza, who wanted to hear more tales about the wealthy cities to the north. Castillo and Dorantes married and settled in Mexico, and Cabeza de Vaca returned to Spain. Estevanico was sold or given to Mendoza, who—with Coronado—organized an expedition north. The exploring party was led by Fray Marcos de Niza, with Estevanico serving as guide. As his group continued north, Fray Marcos sent Estevanico ahead to scout the trail. Estevanico then sent back word to Fray Marcos that he was near "Cibola," seven cities that were rumored to contain fabulous wealth and riches.

Over the next four weeks Marcos chased after Estevanico, but was unable to catch him. Estevanico trekked through the desert and became the first Westerner to enter what is now Arizona and New Mexico. As he traveled, he sent his medicine gourd ahead to announce his arrival. When he reached the pueblo of the Zuni (a Native American tribe) at Hawikuh—the first of the supposed seven cities of Cibola—Estevanico showed his magic gourd. The Zuni chief, however, threw the gourd down in anger and demanded that Estevanico leave the town. Then the chief reversed his orders. Taking away Estevanico's possessions, the chief put him in a house on the edge of town without food or water. The next morning, Estevanico was attacked and killed by a band of warriors. When asked why Estevanico had been killed, the Zuni said Estevanico had claimed that a huge army was coming with weapons. The chiefs met, labeled him a spy, and killed him. Estevanico's body was then cut into little pieces and distributed among the chiefs.

Coronado still had hope of finding treasures, so he sent small exploring parties out into the area. Although his men did not discover gold, they were able to conquer new territory for Spain. For instance, Coronado sent Pedro de Tovar and Fray Juan de Padilla northwest to a province called Tusayan. The men found the ancient villages of the Hopi (a Native American tribe) in what is now northern Arizona. Then they heard about a great river—now called the Colorado River—to the west. The following month Garcia Lopez de Cárdenas led a group in search of the river. When the travelers reached the edge of a great canyon, they saw the Colorado. Not only had they discovered the river, the explorers also became the first Europeans to see the Grand Canyon.

The "Tiguex War"

By late August 1540 the Spaniards were running low on supplies. Now Coronado was in quest not only of gold, but also of food. He sent out another party to the east under the command of Pedro de Alvarado (1485–1541; see "Exploration and Adventure" entry). This group reached the pueblo of Acoma, perched high on a rock, where the inhabitants gave the Spaniards food. Alvarado then went to Tiguex in the Rio Grande valley north of Albuquerque (near present-day Bemalillo). When Alvarado reported back that Tiguex had plenty of food supplies, Coronado decided to make his headquarters there. During the winter of 1540–41, the demands of the Spaniards for supplies and friction over women led to the "Tiguex War." In a confrontation with the Native Americans, the Europeans captured one pueblo and burned two hundred of the residents alive. Several Spaniards were also killed during various engagements, and Coronado was wounded many times.

Coronado is foiled again

Alvarado then traveled to the east to Cicuye (on the Pecos River), where he captured a Plains Indian (perhaps a Pawnee), whom the Spanish named "The Turk." The Turk told stories about the land of Quivira ruled by a powerful king, where there was abundant gold. On April 23, 1541, Coronado left Tiguex to find Quivira and headed eastward into the Great Plains, where the Spanish saw enormous herds of buffalo. When they finally saw the meager material possessions of the nomadic Plains tribes, the Spanish realized they had been duped once again. A frustrated Coronado sent his main force back to the Rio Grand with large supplies of buffalo meat. He then took command of a small detachment that headed north and east for forty-two days, probably reaching central Kansas near the present-day town of Lyons. A member of the party reported that "neither gold nor silver nor any trace of either was found." When the Turk confessed that he had lied in order to draw the Spaniards into the interior, some of the soldiers strangled him to death. (It is said that Coronado opposed his execution.)

Coronado charged with brutality

Now completely defeated, Coronado returned to Tiguex in October 1541. Shortly thereafter he was seriously injured in a riding accident and was near death for some time. By early 1542 the Spaniards were ready to return to Mexico. They left Tiguex in April and arrived in Mexico City in late autumn. Mendoza was angry that the expedition had not resulted in the discovery of treasures, but he gradually came to the view that Coronado had done his best. Mendoza reappointed him governor of New Galicia in 1544.

In May 1544, however, a royal judge began a formal investigation of accusations that Coronado was guilty of brutality to the native people. He was relieved of his duties as governor but was cleared of all charges two years later. He then became an official in the municipal government of Mexico City. In 1547 Coronado testified in favor of Mendoza during an investigation of the viceroy's rule. In reward for his services, he was given a land grant in 1549. Coronado's health continued to decline, however, and he died in Mexico City on September 22, 1554.

FOR FURTHER REFERENCE

Books

Jacobs, William Jay. *Coronado: Dreamer in Golden Armor.* New York City: F. Watts, 1994.

Other

The People. [Videocassette] Public Broadcasting Service (PBS-TV), 1996.

The Many Misadventures of Sir Walter Raleigh

1578 TO 1618

Sir Walter Raleigh was an English soldier, explorer, nobleman, and author who had an adventurous, but ultimately tragic, life. He experienced his first taste of exploration with his half brother, Sir Humphrey Gilbert (c. 1539–1583) on an unsuccessful "voyage of discovery" to North America. From that point onward, Raleigh was virtually at the mercy of Queen Elizabeth I (1533–1603), who became captivated with the young adventurer. Raleigh later organized a colonizing expedition to North America, but this important journey ended in disaster for the "Lost Colony" at Roanoke (see "Exploration and Adventure" entry). When the queen discovered Raleigh had married someone else, she banished him from court.

Fascinated by stories of a mythical place in South America where great wealth could be found, Raleigh led two expeditions to the continent. He was briefly back in the queen's good graces after his bravery in battle at Cádiz, Spain. After Elizabeth I died, however, he was found guilty of treason (treachery against the state) and his life took a downward spiral. Raleigh was so distraught over the charges that he tried to kill himself. Just before Raleigh was to be executed, King James I (1566–1625) gave him a life sentence. While in prison, Raleigh wrote several books, including the first volume of his *History of the World.* He was later released to search for gold in South America. In his final misadventure, Raleigh attacked a Spanish fort against the orders of the king. This act led to Raleigh's arrest, trial, and execution.

Raleigh gains power

Raleigh (who probably spelled his name "Ralegh") was born in the western English county of Devon, the birthplace of many of England's navigators and seamen. In 1578 he sailed on a voyage to North America. The expedition's ships were attacked by the Spanish and had to return without reaching North America in 1579. Following this failure, Raleigh served in Ireland with the English army, which was trying to put down a rebellion aided by the Spanish. In 1581 he was sent to London with dispatches from the army to the court of Queen Elizabeth I, telling her about the battle. Once at court, he immediately caught the queen's eye and soon became her "favorite" and, it is often assumed, her lover.

Sir Walter Raleigh and his son Wat. Raleigh's taste for wealth and adventure often put him at odds with his primary patron, Queen Elizabeth I.

As a result of this royal connection, Raleigh was showered with honors and the chance to become wealthy through holding various offices. He used this position to foster exploration and settlement by the English in North America.

Raleigh gained new-found wealth from a wine monopoly, estates in Ireland, and titled positions. He was therefore able to supply part of the money that Gilbert needed for his expedition to Newfoundland in 1583. Raleigh wanted to go along as well, but was forbidden to do so by the queen. After Gilbert died on his return voyage, Raleigh received a patent (exclusive right) to explore and settle the coast of North America in the queen's name. In April 1584 he dispatched an expedition to present-day North Carolina, which he claimed for England. Upon the return of the expedition, the queen—who was often called the "Virgin Queen" because of her reluctance to marry—gave the newly-claimed area the name "Virginia" for herself.

English queen Elizabeth I financed many of Sir Walter Raleigh's expeditions.

Tragedy strikes in Virginia

Raleigh then wanted to establish a permanent settlement in Virginia, but once again the queen refused him permission to lead the effort himself. In 1585 he sent out an expedition under the command of his cousin, Richard Grenville (1542–1591). The following year the group returned a failure, for not only had they fought with Native Americans, but they had also quarreled among themselves. In 1587 a new expedition departed under the command of John White. White returned to England with the expedition's ships, but he left eighty-nine men, seventeen women, and two children behind.

The next spring Raleigh sent a ship to take supplies to the new colony, which was called Roanoke, but the ship was intercepted by the French and had to return to England. Tragically, it was not until 1591 that another relief expedition was sent. By then it was too late. When the English party arrived, there was no trace of the Roanoke settlement. Raleigh lost a great deal of money in the venture, but this monetary setback paled in comparison to the lives that had apparently been lost at Roanoke. Raleigh's patent expired in 1603.

Searches for El Dorado

In 1588 Raleigh served on the commission that planned England's successful defense against the Spanish Armada (a fleet of swift war ships sent from Spain to invade England). After quarreling with the queen's new favorite, Robert Devereux, the second earl of Essex (1566–1601), however, Raleigh lost some his influence at court. His situation was made even worse when the queen discovered he had been having a relationship with another woman, Elizabeth Throgmorton. The queen had Raleigh imprisoned in the Tower of London in 1592. On his release, Raleigh married Throgmorton and was again banished from court. By this time,

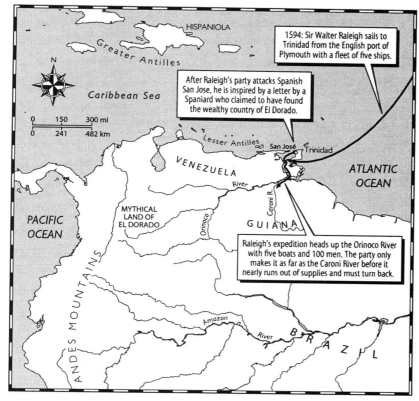

In 1594 Sir Walter Raleigh set sail with a fleet of five ships in search of El Dorado.

Raleigh had become fascinated with Spanish stories of a mythical place called "El Dorado." In 1593 he sent out an expedition under Jacob Whiddon to explore the Orinoco River (in present-day Venezuela) and try to find El Dorado. Returning at the end of the year, Whiddon reported that he could not find the country.

At this point Raleigh decided to set out for El Dorado on his own. He left the English port of Plymouth in early 1594 with a fleet of five ships. He sailed to Trinidad (an island of the present-day West Indies, in the Atlantic Ocean), which was then ruled by the Spanish. After Raleigh's party attacked the town of San Jose, the governor showed him a letter written by a Spaniard who claimed to have found the fabulously wealthy country of El Dorado. On the basis of that evidence, Raleigh and his men went in search of El Dorado themselves. The men cast off on the Orinoco River, then rowed upstream in 5 boats with 100 men. The party went about 125 miles—as far as the Caroni River— but by then they were nearly out of supplies. There had not yet been any signs of El Dorado.

Raleigh left two of the men with a group of natives so that they could learn the language and scout out any traces of El Dorado. He then went back to Trinidad, where he raided other Spanish settlements. Raleigh arrived in England with a load of ore that indeed turned out to contain gold. (Ore is a natural combination of minerals from which metal can be extracted, or taken out. During the nineteenth century, mines for gold and other ores were established in the regions traveled by Raleigh.)

Back in favor

Raleigh was criticized by his enemies at court, who claimed his expedition to South America had been a failure. To justify himself, in 1596 he wrote *Discoverie of Guiana,* which included a map of the area Raleigh had explored. (Guiana is the region between the Orinoco, Negro, and Amazon Rivers.) Raleigh then became involved in preparations for a war against Spain. In 1597 he took part in an English assault on the Spanish port of Cádiz, where he was wounded and distinguished himself by his bravery. Once again in the queen's favor, he was welcomed back to court.

Raleigh attempts suicide

In 1600, Raleigh was appointed Governor of Jersey, one of the Channel Islands in the English Channel off the coast of France. When Elizabeth I died in 1603, however, Raleigh's enemies convinced the new ruler, King James I, that Raleigh was guilty of treason. After being arrested in 1603, Raleigh became so upset that he tried, unsuccessfully, to kill himself. He was then convicted and sentenced to death. Raleigh had actually mounted the scaffold to be beheaded when news came that the king had spared his life. The sentence had been changed to life imprisonment. Raleigh then spent the following thirteen years in the Tower of London (a jail for prominent prisoners), where he lived with his wife and son. During that time he wrote several books, including the first volume of his *History of the World.*

More adventure and misfortune

Starting in 1610, Raleigh argued in favor of sending another expedition to Guiana to look for gold mines. He was released from prison in 1616 in order to lead the expedition, with specific orders not to attack any Spanish settlement. Raleigh mounted the venture with his own money, as well as the investments of several friends. The party left England in June 12, 1617, with a fleet of fourteen ships. The fleet immediately ran into a storm during which one ship sank and many others were damaged. The ships had to put into port in Ireland to make repairs and did not leave again until August.

Throughout the voyage Raleigh faced problems, including a shortage of water, storms, and doldrums (a calm part of the ocean near the Equator) that kept the ships from moving for fourteen days. Raleigh became ill with fever, and many of his men died from illness. Finally anchoring off the coast of what is now French Guiana, the group was able to get fresh water and supplies. Raleigh then sent an old friend, Lawrence Kemys, up the Orinoco River with the main part of the expedition. Among the men were Raleigh's son and his nephew. While Raleigh stayed behind with the ships to guard against a Spanish attack, Kemys and his men attacked San Tomas, a Spanish fort on the Orinoco. During the fighting Raleigh's son was killed. The Spanish abandoned the town, but Kemys would not follow them through the heavy forest. When Kemys returned to Raleigh's ship with the news, he was so severely reprimanded by Raleigh that he committed suicide.

Raleigh executed

Raleigh wanted to pursue the possibility of rich mines in the interior of South America, but by this time none of his men would follow him. The ships parted company, and Raleigh headed north to Newfoundland. He took on a cargo of fish to help pay for the costs of the voyage. He returned to Plymouth in June 1618. By then news of the attack on San Tomas had reached England and the Spanish ambassador insisted that Raleigh should be punished. After he was arrested, Raleigh made an unsuccessful attempt to flee to France. He was put on trial, condemned to death, and executed on October 29, 1618. As Raleigh was about to be beheaded, the executioner wanted him to turn his head another way. His last words were, "What matter how the head lie, so the heart be right?"

FOR FURTHER REFERENCE

Books

Hemming, John. *The Search for El Dorado*. New York City: E. P. Dutton, 1978.

The "Lost Colony" at Roanoke

1588 TO 1591

According to tales told in the late 1500s, a sea dragon or a Gorgon carried the Roanoke settlers away.

The fate of the Roanoke Colony, also known as the "Lost Colony," is one of the most mysterious events in American history. An island off the coast of present-day North Carolina, Roanoke was the site of the earliest attempted English settlement in the New World. (Jamestown, in present-day Virginia, was the first permanent English settlement.) The first colonizing expedition was sponsored in 1585 by famous English soldier, scholar, and adventurer Sir Walter Raleigh (see "Exploration and Adventure" entry). The settlers did not remain long on the island, however, because of conflicts with Native Americans. A second effort to build a colony was made by fifteen Englishmen in 1586, but they disappeared without a trace. Two years later the Roanoke Colony was established by 116 English settlers under the leadership of John White. When White went back to England to gather supplies, he was unexpectedly delayed for almost three years as the Spanish Armada tried unsuccessfully to invade England. Upon arriving at Roanoke in 1591, he found that time had played a cruel trick: the colony had simply vanished. The details surrounding the disappearance of the Roanoke colony were a mystery then and remain so today.

Je Port oder Meerhafen der Landschafft Virginia iſt voll Inſeln/ die da verurſachen/ daß man gar beſchwerlichen in dieſelben kommen kan. Dann wiewol ſie an vielen orten weit von einander geſcheiden ſind/ vnd ſich anſehen läſſet/ als ſolte man dadurch leicht-lich können hinein kommen/ ſo haben wir dannoch mit vnſerm groſſen ſchaden erfahren/ daß dieſelben offne Plätz voll Sandes ſind. Deßwegen haben wir niemals können hin-ein kommen/ biß ſo lang wir an vielen vnnd mancherley örtern mit einem kleinen Schiff die ſach verſucht haben. Zuletzt haben wir einen Paß gefunden/ auff einem ſonderlichen ort/ der vnſern Engelländern wol bekannt iſt. Als wir nun hinein kommen/ vnd eine zeitlang darinn on vn-terlaß geſchifft hatten/ ſind wir eines groſſen flieſſenden Waſſers gewar worden/ deſſen außgang gegen der Inſeln/ von welcher wir geſagt haben/ ſich erſtrecket. Dieweil aber der Inngang zu demſelbigē Waſſer deß Sandes halben zu klein war/ haben wir denſelben verlaſſen/ vñ ſeyn weiter fort geſchifft/ biß daß wir an ei-ne groſſe Inſeln kommen ſind/ deren Einwohner/ nach dem ſie vnſer gewar worden/ haben alsbald mit lau-ter vnd ſchrecklicher ſtinm zu ruffen angefangen/ dieweil ſie zuvor keine Menſchen/ die vns gleich weren/ be-ſchawet hatten. Deßwegen ſie ſich auch auff die Flucht begeben haben/ vnnd nicht anders dann als Wölffe vnd vnſinnige Leut/ alles mit ihrem heulen erfüllt. Da wir ihnen aber freundtlich nachgeruffen/ vnd ſie wi-derumb zu vns gelocket/ auch ihnen vnſere Wahr/ als da ſind Spiegel/ Meſſer/ Puppen/ vnd ander geringe Krämerey (an welchen wir vermeyneten ſie einen luſt haben ſolten) fürgeſtellt hatten/ ſind ſie ſtehen bliebē. Vnd nach dem ſie vnſern guten willen vnd freundtſchafft geſpürt/ haben ſie vns gute Wort geben/ vnnd zu vnſer ankunfft glück gewündſchet. Darnach haben ſie vns in ihre Statt/ Roanoac genannt/ ja daß noch mehr iſt/ zu ihrem Weroans oder Oberherrn geführet/ der vns freundtlich empfangen hat/ wiewol er erſt-lich ſich ab vns entſetzte. Alſo iſt es vns ergangē in vnſer erſten ankunfft der newen Welt/ ſo wir Virginiam nennten. Was nun für Leiber/ Kleydung/ art zu leben/ Feſte vnd Gaſtereyen die Einwohner daſelbſt haben/ das wil ich ſtück für ſtück nach einander einem jeden vor die Augen ſtellen/ wie nachfolget.

Settlers face starvation

The story of Roanoke began when a group of English settlers sponsored by Raleigh convinced Queen Elizabeth I (1533–1603) to support a colony in the New World (a name given by Europeans to North and South America). Not only did Raleigh have great influence over the queen, but Elizabeth I was also eager to claim land in the New World before the Spanish. In 1585 Richard Grenville (1542–1591), a cousin of Raleigh, and Ralph Lane, who was to be governor of the new settlement, set out with 107 colonists. Also in the party were German scientist Joachim Ganz and English mathematician Thomas Harriot (1560–1621), who wrote *A Brief and True Report of the New Found Land of Virginia* in 1588. The men's goal was to find copper and other precious metals, and the experiments performed by Ganz and Harriot would later provide insight into the mystery that now surrounds Roanoke.

At first, the Europeans had good relations with the native Algonquin tribe. Soon, however, the relationship was tested. A substantial amount of the English provisions had been lost at sea, so the settlers' food supply was low. Since they knew little about farming, the colonists did not know how to grow their own food. The Algonquins offered kindness and generosity, supplying the settlers with food and teaching them how to survive on the land. In the meantime, Grenville had gone back to England for more supplies. As the settlers became more desperate, however, they began demanding food from the native people. When Grenville was late in returning, Lane became worried about the mounting tensions between the settlers and the tribe. Suspecting the tribe's chief, Wingina, was threatening upheaval, Lane and his men attacked and beheaded the tribal leader. Not only were the colonists facing starvation, but they had now invited outright conflict with the Algonquins.

When English explorer Francis Drake (c. 1543–1596) arrived in June 1586, the settlers demanded that he take them back to England. They were so eager to depart that they left behind three men, who were never heard from again. Only two days after the settlers had set out for England, one of Grenville's vessels finally came with supplies and 600 more men. The new arrivals found no one at the colony. Although this most recent

◄ An early map of the Roanoke colony.

group decided not to stay, they left behind fifteen men to guard the fort the previous settlers had built as a lookout for Spanish and French ships.

A third group lands at Roanoke

In 1587 Raleigh and White organized a third colonizing expedition that would be headed by White. By this time, eighteen lives had been lost at Roanoke. Raleigh and White decided that for a colony to be successful in the New World, it would need families, not just soldiers, to cultivate and settle the land. An enticement was needed, however, because of the poor results of their efforts thus far. Raleigh therefore offered 500 acres of land and promised all participants a voice in the government of the new colony. Tempted by these attractions, 116 pioneers left the security of their lives in England for the excitement and challenges of the New World.

Like the English settlers bound for the New World two years earlier, White and his group experienced hardships at sea. One of the ships carrying their food supply was lost during a severe storm. White planned to establish his colony in the Chesapeake Bay area, but first he needed to stop at Roanoke to check on Grenville's men at the fort. As the ships made the scheduled detour to the island, the captain refused to take the settlers any farther. Historians speculate that the captain and his crew were privateers who were impatient to go down to the West Indies and steal goods from ships—a more lucrative prospect than transporting settlers. Now stranded, White and his party stepped onto Roanoke only to discover that Grenville's men had disappeared. The men had enough supplies for two years, but it is not known how long they actually lived. Only one skeleton remained at the site.

With prospects already bleak, the colonists had to endure a long, harsh winter. In the spring White was chosen to return to England for supplies. Only nine days before White's departure, his granddaughter, Virginia Dare, was born to his daughter, Eleanor, and son-in-law, Ananias Dare. Baby Virginia was the first European known to be born in America. White had intended on a quick return with essential supplies, but he arrived to find his country at war with Spain. It would be three years before he would come back to Roanoke. When White arrived in England, Raleigh was no longer in the queen's good graces and showed little interest in the people at Roanoke. White realized that the key men in the establishment of this new colony could do nothing for the settlement an ocean away. Their main concern was defending England from the Spanish.

The colony had vanished

When White finally returned to Roanoke in 1591, he must have felt an eerie horror at discovering the disappearance of the whole colony. Not only had his daughter, son-in-law, and four-year-old granddaughter been lost, but a host of other families as well. White's only clues were the word "Croatoan," which had been carved onto a fence post and the letters "Cro" on a tree trunk. The most immediate suspicion was that the colonists' disappearance was somehow linked with the Croatoan, a friendly Native American tribe who lived on Croatoan Island about fifty miles south of Roanoke. But White died without ever actually knowing what happened to his family.

What happened to the Roanoke colony?

Scholars have been able only to speculate about the fate of the pioneers at Roanoke. Natural possibilities at the time included disease and starvation or weather-related devastation, such as a hurricane, flood, fire, or tornado. The colonists could have tried to return to England and their ship sank at sea or they may have been invaded by another country striving to establish its place in the New World. Other, more outlandish theories include pirates coming ashore and kidnaping all the Roanoke inhabitants. There have even been unbelievable tales of a sea dragon or a Gorgon (one of three snake-haired sisters in Greek mythology) carrying the settlers away. However absurd these thoughts may seem now, they were not uncommon in the sixteenth century.

The most positive and reassuring conclusion is that Virginia Dare and the rest of the colony joined a Native American tribe and prospered. Today, it is thought that the group went north to the Chesapeake Bay area where Raleigh originally wanted them to settle. Regardless of the explanations, the fate of the people at Roanoke is still and may always be an unsettling mystery. The disappearance and possible tragedy that befell the settlement was later commemorated by two stamps. In 1937 President Franklin D. Roosevelt (1882–1945) drew a design for one—the Virginia Dare stamp—which marked the three hundred fiftieth anniversary of Dare's birth. Dare is the youngest person officially honored on a U.S. postage stamp.

Roanoke legacy

The people of Roanoke laid the groundwork for the ultimate prosperity of Jamestown, the first permanent English settlement in the New World, established in Virginia twenty-two years later. The colonists' courage and determination in venturing to the unknown New World was an inspiration to other settlers. The Algonquians must also be recognized for their generosity in sharing knowledge about farming with the new arrivals. This alliance between Native Americans and arriving Europeans led to the ultimate survival of later colonies in the New World.

FOR FURTHER REFERENCE

Books

Campbell, Elizabeth A. *The Carving in the Tree.* New York City: Little, Brown, 1968.

Periodicals

Steven, William K. "Drought May Have Doomed the Lost Colony," *The New York Times.* April 24, 1998, pp. A1, A14.

Warrick, Joby. "Trees Hold Clues to Jamestown Mystery." *Washington Post.* April 24, 1998, p. AO3.

Willem Barents's Search for a Northeast Passage

1596 TO 1597

After Barents died, the Dutch ended their search for a northeast passage.

When Dutch navigator Willem Barents set out on his final voyage in 1596, he was making his third attempt to find a northeast passage to Asia as part of the Dutch Arctic Enterprise. On all three northeast passage expeditions, Barents was the chief pilot (the person who charts the route the ship will take). On Barents's first two journeys, the expeditions' success had been halted by monstrous chunks of pack ice that stopped any forward motion of the parties' ships. Barents remained persistent, however, and set out one last time. On this last trek Barents was the pilot for an expedition led by Jacob van Heemskerck (1597–1656). The explorers succeeded in rounding the northern tip of Novaya Zemlya (two large islands in the Arctic Ocean, off the northeast coast of Russia), but again got stuck in the ice. After spending the winter onboard ship, Barents and his crew started for the mainland in two small boats. Barents died along the way.

Dutch seek route

Willem Barents (also called "Harefflazoon," or "Barent's son,") was a native of the island of Ter Schelling off the coast of Friesland in the northern Netherlands. Barents moved to Amsterdam and became a burgher (middle-class citizen) of that city. In 1594 Barents was commissioned by Dutch merchants to

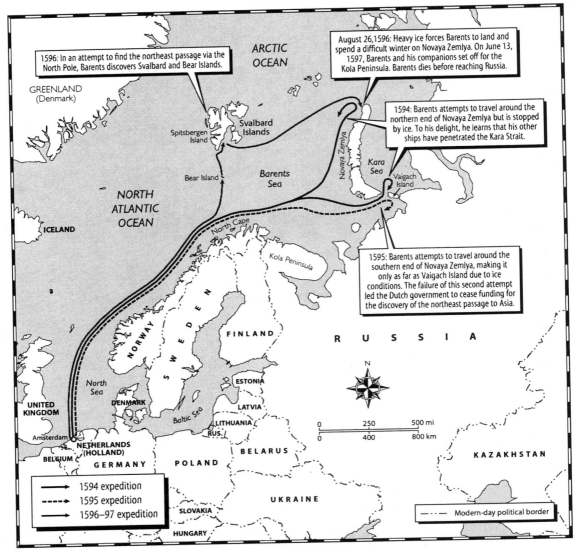

1596: In an attempt to find the northeast passage via the North Pole, Barents discovers Svalbard and Bear Islands.

August 26,1596: Heavy ice forces Barents to land and spend a difficult winter on Novaya Zemlya. On June 13, 1597, Barents and his companions set off for the Kola Peninsula. Barents dies before reaching Russia.

1594: Barents attempts to travel around the northern end of Novaya Zemlya but is stopped by ice. To his delight, he learns that his other ships have penetrated the Kara Strait.

1595: Barents attempts to travel around the southern end of Novaya Zemlya, making it only as far as Vaigach Island due to ice conditions. The failure of this second attempt led the Dutch government to cease funding for the discovery of the northeast passage to Asia.

ARCTIC OCEAN

GREENLAND (Denmark)

Spitsbergen Island

Svalbard Islands

Bear Island

Barents Sea

Novaya Zemlya

Kara Sea

Vaigach Island

NORTH ATLANTIC OCEAN

ICELAND

North Cape

Kola Peninsula

NORWAY

SWEDEN

FINLAND

RUSSIA

North Sea

DENMARK

ESTONIA

LATVIA

LITHUANIA

RUS.

Baltic Sea

BELARUS

KAZAKHSTAN

UNITED KINGDOM

Amsterdam

NETHERLANDS (HOLLAND)

BELGIUM

GERMANY

POLAND

UKRAINE

SLOVAKIA

HUNGARY

N

0 — 250 — 500 mi
0 — 400 — 800 km

1594 expedition
1595 expedition
1596–97 expedition

------- Modern-day political border

Dutch navigator Willem Barents made three attempt to find a northeast passage to Asia.

lead an expedition to China, which began his successful journeys to the Arctic.

At the end of the sixteenth century, merchants in the Netherlands were among the most enterprising tradesmen in the world. Their chief interest was in breaking the monopoly of trade with Asia, which was held by the Portuguese and the Spanish. At the time, most trade was conducted via a southern route around Africa controlled by Portugal, and between the

Philippines and Mexico, which was sailed by Spanish galleons (ships used for trade and war). Although the Dutch were trying to force their way into this established southern route, they reasoned that there must be a way north as well—a northeast passage. The Dutch initiated a series of voyages designed to sail north of Eurasia (the name then given to Europe and Asia as a single continent) to the northeast tip of Asia and then south into the Pacific Ocean. While the theory was certainly correct, the Dutch seriously underestimated the difficulties involved in finding the route.

Barents begins his first voyage

Commissioned by Dutch merchants to lead an expedition in search of the northeast passage, Barents set sail on June 4, 1594, with four ships. His party embarked from the island of Texel north of Amsterdam and headed through the North Sea. China was Barents's ultimate destination, so he planned to travel via Novaya Zemlya, off the Arctic coast of European Russia. Barents sailed north of Norway through the sea that is now named after him. He and his party made it as far as the northern tip of Novaya Zemlya. The ships could proceed no farther, however, because of the pack ice that lay for miles ahead. Crew member Gerrit de Veer wrote that the ice looked like "a plain field." When Barents turned around to go back by the same route he found, to his delight, that his other ships had penetrated the Kara Strait (a waterway that connects the Kara Sea with the Barents Sea). Barents had earlier avoided this area because of reports that a massive ice barrier stretched across its entrance.

Second voyage also fails

Accessing the Kara Strait was a great stride in the navigation of a northeast passage. If the Dutch would have pressed on, they might well have reached the waterway that connects the Arctic Ocean with the Bering Sea, a channel now called the Bering Strait. In the meantime, a companion voyage by Jan van Linschoten (1563-1611) was able to reach the Kara Sea east of Novaya Zemlya by sailing south of the island. It was by this route that Barents and Linschoten sailed on a second expedition. The ice was so bad, however, that the group traveled only as far as Vaigach Island, which is in the straits between Novaya Zemlya and the mainland.

Barents's ship is crushed by ice

On May 13, 1596, Barents set out again, this time as pilot for an expedition of two ships led by van Heemskerck. Along the way the crew discovered Svalbard and Bear Island, north of Norway, and rounded the northern tip of Novaya Zemlya. One of the ships turned back to Amsterdam, but van Heemskerck and Barents stayed behind. On the north coast of Novaya Zemlya the ice closed in and gradually crushed the little Dutch ship. The men used timber from the vessel to build a shelter on the island. There they spent a terrible winter, which was so cold that the sheets froze on the beds and the wine turned to ice. The men almost suffocated from the smoke of the fire they had to keep burning all the time. By the new year, scurvy (a disease caused by lack of vitamin C) had set in and one crewman had died. The ice was piled high around the ship. According to de Veer, it was "as if there had been whole towns made of ice."

Willem Barents died of cold and exposure after he and his crew tried to sail longboats from the island of Novaya Zemlya to the mainland.

When spring came, Barents decided that the remaining men's only chance was to sail in the longboats from the ship to the nearest mainland, the Kola Peninsula, sixteen hundred miles away. (A longboat was a very large rowboat used on merchant ships.) The crew started out, rowing through rough water and dangerous ice. Remarkably, the men reached their destination. This accomplishment was bittersweet, however, because Barents did not arrive with them. He had died of cold and exposure along the way. Although most of Barents's companions survived, this was the last attempt the Dutch made to find a northeast passage.

Expedition finds remains

Barents's story did not end on the Kola Peninsula. Nearly three hundred years after the explorer's death, in 1871, a Norwegian expedition found the remains of Barents's winter quarters. Among the scattered contents were pots, swords, gun barrels, flutes, drumsticks, a Dutch clock, and paintings. In 1875 another explorer found part of Barents's journal, which provides a good record of the first winter spent in the Arctic by Europeans. Also among Barents's legacies were navigational charts and meteorological data that are still consulted today. Consequently, Barents's final voyage can be seen as both a misadventure and a success. His heroic but futile attempts to find a northeast passage brought an end to Dutch plans for breaking the Portuguese-Spanish trade monopoly. Yet as a result of his accomplishments on the expeditions, he is ranked among the most important arctic explorers.

FOR FURTHER REFERENCE

Books

Kirwan, L. P. *A History of Polar Exploration.* New York City: Norton, 1959.

The Downfall of René-Robert de La Salle

1687

After a series of disastrous setbacks, La Salle was murdered by his own men.

René-Robert de La Salle was a celebrated French explorer who made great strides in the exploration of North America. As a young man, La Salle joined a religious order. He later left the seminary, however, and became an important builder of New France (modern Canada). After receiving patents (exclusive right) to explore, trade, and construct forts by the French government, La Salle and his men set out across the Great Lakes in a specially built ship called the *Griffon* in 1679. In the following years, La Salle's group established the sites of many present-day cities in the Midwest; La Salle also became the first European to sail down the Mississippi River to its mouth. In spite of La Salle's successes, however, he was also responsible for several misadventures and disasters that resulted in his murder at the hands of his own men.

Studies for priesthood

La Salle was born in 1643 into a well-to-do family in Rouen, the capital of the French province of Normandy. He studied at a school run by Jesuits (a Roman Catholic religious order) in his hometown. La Salle then became a novice (a student who is studying for the Catholic priesthood) at a Jesuit seminary in Paris. He showed an aptitude for mathematics and taught that subject to secondary school students while pursuing his own studies. La Salle was not a successful seminarian, however, because the Jesuits thought he was too adventurous and unstable. After being turned down twice for a chance to be a missionary, he quit his religious studies in 1667.

La Salle had family connections in New France, so he moved to Quebec sometime later that year. He was granted a gift of land on the island of Montreal (located on the St. Lawrence River in Canada) and sold it two years later for a profit. With this money La Salle decided to lead an expedition to find the Ohio River, which he thought would lead to the South Seas and eventually to China.

La Salle's first expedition a disaster

With La Salle's new profits, the expedition to find the Ohio River became a reality in 1669. As the party set out from Montreal it attracted the attention of the Sulpicians, a Catholic order that sent along two of its members to serve as missionaries. Since none of the group had any exploring experience, the trip turned into a disaster. The men crossed Lake Ontario and then were forced to spend a month in the village of a hostile Seneca tribe. They were finally rescued by an Iroquois tribesman who offered to guide them to the Ohio by way of Lake Erie. But before the expedition got as far as Lake Erie, La Salle became sick with fever and the two missionaries were lured away to visit the Potawatomi tribe.

Because of his illness, La Salle told his companions he was going to return to Montreal. He did not turn up there again, however, until the fall of 1673. There is no record of La Salle's travels from 1669 to 1670, but many later supporters claimed that he discovered the Ohio and Mississippi Rivers. Evidence shows that this is almost certainly not true and that the Mississippi was not found until 1673 by the French explorers Louis Jolliet (1645–1700) and Jacques Marquette (1637–1675).

Disappears for two years

Historians do not know where La Salle traveled during the next two years. Records show that in the fall of 1673 he returned to Montreal, where he gained power and prominence. He sided with Louis de Buade (1622–1698; also known as the Count of Frontenac), the governor of New

France, in a dispute that was then going on in the colony. As a result, La Salle was rewarded with a title of nobility, Sieur de La Salle, and command of Fort Frontenac at the site of present-day Kingston, Ontario. In 1677 he went back to France, and the following year he received permission from the king to explore the western part of North America between New France, Florida, and Mexico.

Explores vast territories

La Salle had reached his goal. He now had the authority to explore a vast region in the New World. La Salle started his expedition by constructing a fort on the Niagara River between the area that is now Ontario in Canada and the state of New York. He was accompanied by several other French explorers who were to gain fame as well, including Henry de Tonti (1650–1704) and Louis Hennepin (1626–c. 1701). La Salle was forced to spend the winter of 1678–79 at Fort Frontenac. Upon his return he discovered that his men had built a ship, called the *Griffon*, to explore the Great Lakes. The crew sailed on August 7, 1679.

The explorers traveled through Lake Erie into Lake Huron and then to Michilimackinac, a strip of land that separates Lake Huron from Lake Michigan. Leaving the *Griffon*, the group went south on Lake Michigan in canoes. In the middle of winter they reached a village of the Illinois tribe near the present-day city of Peoria, Illinois. When the Illinois discouraged them about proceeding farther, several of La Salle's men deserted the mission. La Salle built a fort called Crèvecoeur in the area to serve as a supply center for future explorations. Before heading back to Canada, La Salle sent Hennepin to lead an advance party to the Mississippi.

Disaster at Crèavecoeur

La Salle's return trip to Canada was beset by disaster after disaster. The *Griffon* got lost, La Salle discovered the fort on the Niagara had been burned down, and one of his supply ships sank. After reaching Montreal in June 1680, La Salle started back to Crèvecoeur. At Fort Frontenac he learned that the supply center had been burned. Hearing that news, many of La Salle's men deserted and started back to Canada. Along the way they robbed their former leader's supply posts. In hot pursuit

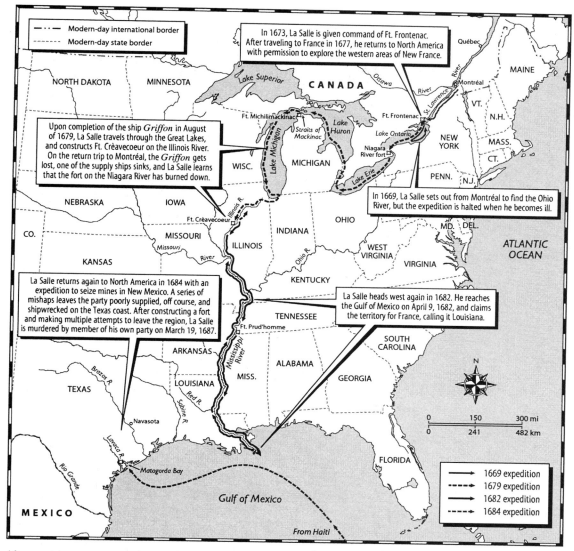

In 1673, La Salle is given command of Ft. Frontenac. After traveling to France in 1677, he returns to North America with permission to explore the western areas of New France.

Upon completion of the ship *Griffon* in August of 1679, La Salle travels through the Great Lakes, and constructs Ft. Crèavecoeur on the Illinois River. On the return trip to Montréal, the *Griffon* gets lost, one of the supply ships sinks, and La Salle learns that the fort on the Niagara River has burned down.

In 1669, La Salle sets out from Montréal to find the Ohio River, but the expedition is halted when he becomes ill.

La Salle returns again to North America in 1684 with an expedition to seize mines in New Mexico. A series of mishaps leaves the party poorly supplied, off course, and shipwrecked on the Texas coast. After constructing a fort and making multiple attempts to leave the region, La Salle is murdered by member of his own party on March 19, 1687.

La Salle heads west again in 1682. He reaches the Gulf of Mexico on April 9, 1682, and claims the territory for France, calling it Louisiana.

Modern-day international border
Modern-day state border

1669 expedition
1679 expedition
1682 expedition
1684 expedition

After receiving patents to explore, trade, and construct forts by the French government, René-Robert de La Salle and his men set out on a number of exploratory expeditions.

of the deserters, La Salle set an ambush and captured them. He then retraced his route and went all the way back to Crèavecoeur. La Salle hoped to find Tonti, who he had left in charge. Upon reaching the burned fort, La Salle found that Tonti was not among the bodies. When the two explorers finally met the following May, La Salle discovered that Tonti had returned by canoe to Michilimackinac.

In 1681 La Salle returned once again to Montreal. His most important task was to calm his creditors, as well as silence his enemies, who were spreading rumors about La Salle's mismanagement of the expedition. After a brief and apparently successful stay, La Salle headed back into the wilderness with a party of about forty men. Reaching Fort Crèavecoeur in January 1682, the men set out for the Mississippi the following month. They built canoes and paddled down the river, passing the mouth of the Missouri River. La Salle eventually sighted the Ohio River, which had been the explorer's goal when he set out on his first expedition thirteen years earlier. He later built a fort called Prud'homme on the site of present-day Memphis, Tennessee.

Uneasy peace with Native Americans

The following month, La Salle and his men were almost attacked by a party from the Arkansas tribe. La Salle managed to avoid the conflict and take possession of the country in the name of King Louis XIV of France. The expedition's luck continued to hold as its members found yet more new land. Passing the farthest point reached by Jolliet and Marquette, the men spent time among the Tensas and Natchez tribes. La Salle's party reached the Gulf of Mexico on April 9, 1682. La Salle claimed the territory for France, calling it "Louisiana" in the French king's name. As the group started back upriver the next day, however, they were attacked by Native Americans and La Salle was injured. Remaining at Fort Prud'homme to recuperate, La Salle sent Tonti on ahead to report back to the governor of New France on their discoveries. After a five-month recovery period, La Salle was able to travel as far as Michilimackinac, where he met Tonti and sent dispatches on his successful ventures to Quebec and to France.

Misrepresents discoveries

More trouble was in store for La Salle. While he was recovering from his illness, a new governor had arrived in New France. The governor was quickly influenced by La Salle's enemies, who charged the explorer with mismanagement of the expedition and mistreatment of his men. On the governor's orders, La Salle was sent back to France in December 1683 to report on his conduct. In addition to having to account for himself, La Salle found there was very little support in France for his ideas about developing the Mississippi Valley, and he was eventually relieved of his authority.

La Salle managed to make the best of the situation. He learned that an influential group was trying to interest the French government in sending an expedition to the mouth of the Rio Grande in the Gulf of Mexico. The group's plan was to seize valuable mines in New Mexico and New Spain (present-day Mexico). In order to be part of these schemes, La Salle purposely lied about his discoveries, virtually moving the Mississippi River from Louisiana to Texas. He made a map that depicted the Mississippi River as being much farther to the west and emptying into the Gulf of Mexico from Texas rather than Louisiana.

Doomed quest for Gulf of Mexico

With his falsified document, La Salle was able to convince the king and rich French merchants to sponsor an expedition to the Gulf of Mexico. La Salle left France at the end of July in 1684 as the head of an expedition of 4 ships and 327 men and women. As a result of bad planning and La Salle's ongoing quarrel with the ships' captain, the boats were overloaded and there was not enough water. The ships were forced to stop at the French colony of Haiti (an island in the Caribbean Sea). There the men learned that one of their ships, which was carrying most of the expedition's supplies, had been captured by the Spanish. Leaving Haiti with the three remaining ships in November, La Salle headed toward the Mississippi delta. (A delta is a triangular deposit of sand, gravel, clay, and similar materials found at the mouth of a river.) On December 27 and 28, La Salle's party saw muddy waters that indicated they were near the mouth of the great river. La Salle, however, had made miscalculations in his navigation and chose to believe unreliable old Spanish charts.

Instead of investigating the immediate area, La Salle decided he was much farther east than he actually was and began to head west. At this point the expedition's fortunes took a downward spiral. By the time La Salle realized his mistake, his ships were off Matagorda Bay south of the site of present-day Houston, Texas. While trying to get into the bay, however, one of the ships ran aground (got stuck in shallow water). Local natives tried to take some of the goods from the wrecked ship and the Frenchmen shot at them. From then on, the two groups were enemies. The crisis became even more serious in March, when the naval captain for the expedition returned to France with one of the ships. Many of La Salle's men, who by now had become discouraged, went with the captain. La Salle was left behind with only one boat and a very unhappy exploring party.

La Salle killed in cold blood

In May 1685 La Salle tried to salvage the expedition. He constructed a fort at the mouth of the Lavaca River on Matagorda Bay. From there, he and several members of the party made exploring trips into the surrounding countryside. Disaster struck the following spring. The group's last ship was wrecked when the pilot became drunk, leaving the little colony without any means of escape. La Salle decided the only way out was to travel overland to the Mississippi and then head up the river to the Great Lakes, where they could find French missions and traders. The party of twenty men left at the end of April. As a result of various mishaps, the number was reduced to eight by October. La Salle was forced to return to the fort on the Lavaca.

La Salle set out again in January 1687 with seventeen companions, leaving twenty-five men behind at the fort. By this time the men hated La Salle for causing them such misery. On the night of March 18 or 19, 1687, a group of five men killed La Salle's nephew, servant, and guide. The next morning, at a spot just north of the modern town of Navasota, Texas, the members of the group shot La Salle in cold blood and left his body for wild animals to eat. The remaining members of La Salle's party reached Montreal on July 13, 1688.

FOR FURTHER REFERENCE

Books

Coulter, Tony. *La Salle and the Explorers of the Mississippi.* New York City: Chelsea House, 1991.

Terrell, John Upton. *The Life and Times of an Explorer.* London, England: Weybright and Talley, 1968.

James Cook in the South Pacific and Antarctica

1768 TO 1780

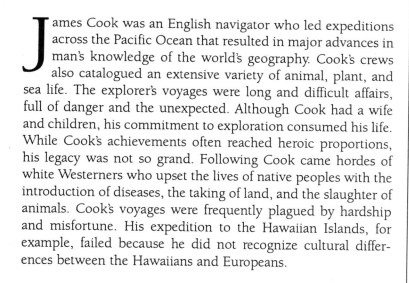

James Cook was an English navigator who led expeditions across the Pacific Ocean that resulted in major advances in man's knowledge of the world's geography. Cook's crews also catalogued an extensive variety of animal, plant, and sea life. The explorer's voyages were long and difficult affairs, full of danger and the unexpected. Although Cook had a wife and children, his commitment to exploration consumed his life. While Cook's achievements often reached heroic proportions, his legacy was not so grand. Following Cook came hordes of white Westerners who upset the lives of native peoples with the introduction of diseases, the taking of land, and the slaughter of animals. Cook's voyages were frequently plagued by hardship and misfortune. His expedition to the Hawaiian Islands, for example, failed because he did not recognize cultural differences between the Hawaiians and Europeans.

Following Cook came hordes of white Westerners who devastated the lives of native peoples with the introduction of diseases, the taking of land, and the slaughter of animals.

Sent on secret mission to Great Southern Continent

In 1768 the Royal Society asked the British government to send a ship to the Pacific to study the movement of the planet Venus across the Sun. The ultimate purpose of the expedition was to help calculate the distance from the Sun to the Earth. The island of Tahiti was chosen as the best spot for the observation. A secret part of Cook's mission, however, was to investi-

James Cook lands in the New Hebrides. During their travels Cook's crews catalogued an extensive variety of animal, plant, and sea life.

gate the Great Southern Continent that was thought to exist in the South Pacific. For the expedition Cook was given command of the *Endeavour,* a converted collier (a coal-carrying ship). During the voyage Cook found nothing before reaching Tahiti on April 11, 1769. At that time there was still no accurate way of calculating longitude (the angular distance from the prime meridian in Greenwich, England—north and south on the globe) and Cook had to find the island by reaching its latitude (the angular distance north or south of the equator—east-west on the globe) and then sailing west until he ran into it.

Cook encounters culture clash

Cook spent three months in Tahiti, establishing the first prolonged contact between Tahitians and Westerners. He built a little fort, called Fort Venus, at the eastern side of Matavai Bay. Cook had instructed everyone under his command to treat the population "with every imaginable humanity." Yet the

AN ISLAND PARADISE A tiny island in the Pacific Ocean, Tahiti is thirty-three miles long, with an area of less than forty thousand square miles. Cook considered Tahiti a paradise, full of natural wonders. A mountain range rising to seven thousand feet divided the island. Flowers and fruit grew everywhere, and the warm temperatures made life quite comfortable. The island was free of snakes and wild animals. The native inhabitants had smooth brown skin, dark eyes, and perfect teeth. They were exceptionally beautiful, especially the young women. Older Tahitians tended to be overweight, and their bodies were marked by lampblack tattoos on their legs and buttocks.

Tahitians did not have to work much since their food supply was so plentiful. Their teeth did not decay, and they did not become sick. They were exceptionally clean and bathed three times a day. Tahitians lived with no sense of shame, and young Tahitian girls were sexually promiscuous (they had sexual relations with more than one partner. Older women, however, were monogamous, or sexually active with one partner). A social structure divided Tahitians into tribes, with each tribe having an upper class and lower class that consisted of servants. Yet not everything was perfect in this paradise. Just before Cook's arrival a tribal war involving the entire society was fought between Big Tahiti and Little Tahiti. In addition, Tahitian priests practiced infanticide (the killing of babies) as a means of self-preservation.

When Cook landed on Tahiti, forty thousand natives lived on the island. Fifty years later, however, the population had dropped to fewer than ten thousand and life had changed drastically—a direct result of Cook's establishing contact between Tahiti and the Western world.

Europeans and Tahitians had different ideas about the ownership of property that would lead to a misunderstanding. The Tahitians felt compelled to steal from the British, and the British felt equally compelled to get their things back. There was no middle ground. On the Europeans' first visit, for instance, a spyglass and snuff box belonging to the scientist Joseph Banks were stolen, and he demanded them back. When a midshipman gave the order to fire upon an islander who had run off with a musket, the stealing had reached a serious level of concern. The native was shot dead, so other Tahitians thought it best to hide from the white men. The stealing continued, reaching a crisis for Cook when a quadrant (an instrument for measuring altitudes) he needed for the astronomical observations was stolen. Luckily, the quadrant was returned. The transit of Venus was observed (although the observations did not help in making the desired calculations), the coast of the island was charted, and the *Endeavour* sailed on July 12, 1769.

Has disastrous contact with Maoris

Cook visited neighboring islands, which he named the Society Islands in honor of the Royal Society. His crew then sailed south without seeing any large landmass that could be the Great Southern Continent. Cook took a zigzag course to the west until he sighted the east coast of New Zealand's North Island on October 6, 1769. Cook's relations with New Zealand Maoris (native peoples) were not as successful as his dealing with the Tahitians. The Maori would not let Cook's men send a boat ashore, and in the ensuing struggle, four Maoris were killed. Distressed that his contact with native New Zealanders had ended so badly, Cook continued on his voyage. As he was charting the coastline, he came to the strait that showed New Zealand was made up of two large islands (now called North Island and South Island). The strait was named Cook Strait.

Endeavour almost sinks

After circumnavigating the islands for six months to determine they were not part of a continental landmass, Cook headed home. Nearly three weeks later, on April 19, 1770, he sighted the southeast corner of mainland Australia. He found an anchorage at Botany Bay, south of present-day Sydney. There he had his first meeting with the Australian aborigines, who wanted to avoid all contact with Europeans. As the *Endeavour* left Botany Bay and headed out to sea, Cook discovered Moreton Bay, the site of present-day Brisbane. Soon the *Endeavour* was within the treacherous waters of the Great Barrier Reef. (A reef is a chain of rocks or coral or a ridge of sand at or near the surface of water.)

The farther north Cook sailed, the more dangerous the waters became. For weeks the *Endeavour* moved slowly while boats were sent ahead to take soundings (determine the depth of the water), and men on yardarms (long poles that support sails) tried to spot the reefs from above. After successfully sailing a thousand miles, the ship struck a reef and was stalled for more than a day. When the second high tide floated it off, the crew had to work all of the pumps constantly to keep the ship from sinking. Cook was finally forced to "fother" the *Endeavour,* a procedure by which a sail was filled with rags, wool, rope ends, and manure and then passed under the ship to plug the

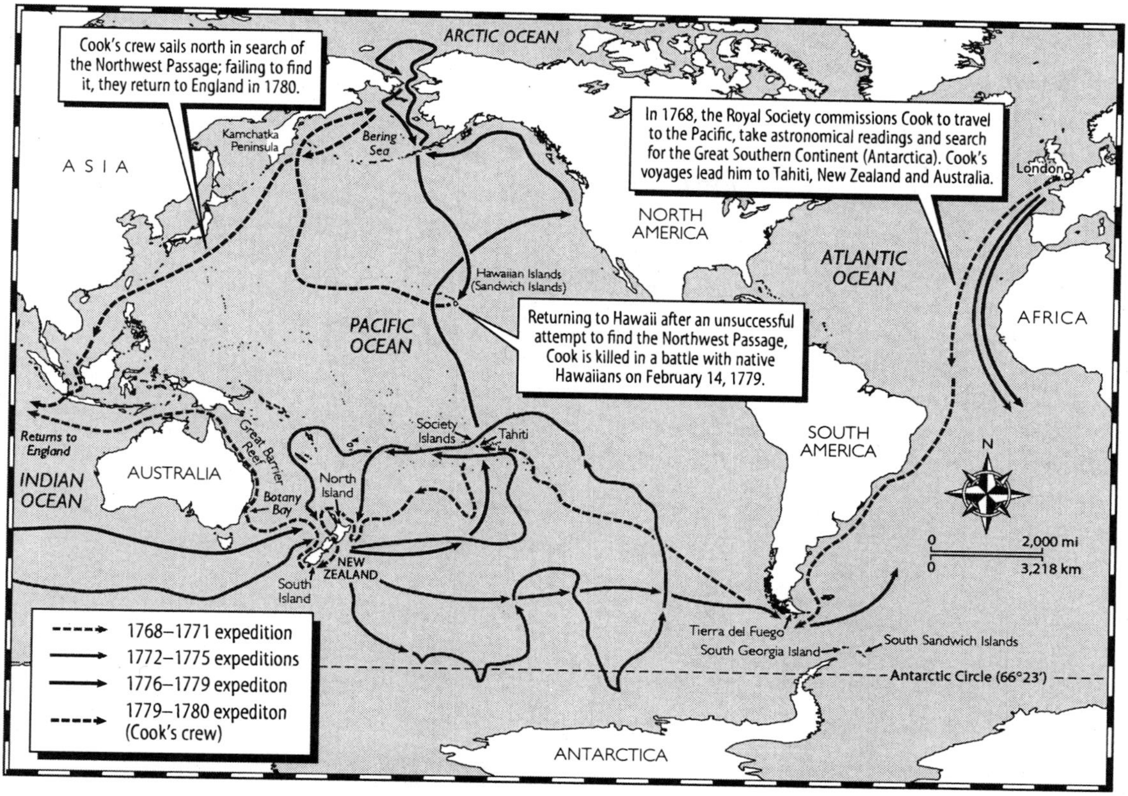

Cook's crew sails north in search of the Northwest Passage; failing to find it, they return to England in 1780.
In 1768, the Royal Society commissions Cook to travel to the Pacific, take astronomical readings and search for the Great Southern Continent (Antarctica). Cook's voyages lead him to Tahiti, New Zealand and Australia.
Returning to Hawaii after an unsuccessful attempt to find the Northwest Passage, Cook is killed in a battle with native Hawaiians on February 14, 1779.
ARCTIC OCEAN
ASIA
Kamchatka Peninsula
Bering Sea
London
NORTH AMERICA
ATLANTIC OCEAN
Hawaiian Islands (Sandwich Islands)
PACIFIC OCEAN
AFRICA
Society Islands
Tahiti
SOUTH AMERICA
Returns to England
INDIAN OCEAN
AUSTRALIA
Great Barrier Reef
Botany Bay
North Island
NEW ZEALAND
South Island
N
0 2,000 mi
0 3,218 km
Tierra del Fuego
South Georgia Island
South Sandwich Islands
Antarctic Circle (66°23')
ANTARCTICA
1768–1771 expedition
1772–1775 expeditions
1776–1779 expediton
1779–1780 expediton (Cook's crew)

James Cook led expeditions across the Pacific Ocean that resulted in major advances in man's knowledge of the world's geography.

hole. (Fothering is comparable to putting a giant bandage on a ship.) After freeing the vessel, the crew reached safety at the mouth of a small river, which was later named the Endeavour River. There Cook discovered that a large piece of coral was caught in the *Endeavour*'s hole, which had probably kept the ship from sinking. The party stayed at the mouth of the river for six weeks, until early August, 1770, making repairs.

Cook studies the Australian Aborigines

The layover gave Cook more time to become better acquainted with the Aborigines, who were physically and temperamentally different from the Tahitians. Little was known of Australia, then called New Holland, at the time of Cook's visit. The Aborigines existed in harmony with nature. They did not wear clothes or live in houses, and they were not interested in

THE FATE OF THE ABORIGINES

The fate of the Aborigines after Cook's departure from Australia was not happy. The Australian Aborigines had no concept of private property. This trait left them completely vulnerable to European greed. Within fifty years, the British had taken over the country, introducing European crops, farm animals, and trees. Unable to conform to foreign customs, the Aborigines were pushed out of the way by masses of white settlers. Foreign diseases killed most of the native peoples. Prostitution among aboriginal women resulted in their becoming sterile or producing half-castes (people of mixed race who had inferior social status) who were wanted by neither group. The Aborigines did not understand English law, so they had no way of knowing that the British were taking their land.

According to Alan Morehead, author of *Fatal Impact,* a book about the effects of Cook's voyages on native peoples in the Pacific and Australia, scientist Charles Darwin was appalled by what European settlers had done to Australia. When Darwin visited Sydney in 1836, he wrote: "Wherever the European has trod death seems to pursue the aboriginal. We may look to the wide extent of the Americas, Polynesia, the Cape of Good Hope and Australia, and we find the same result." English explorer Edward John Eyre (1815–1901; known as the "Protector of the Aborigines") also wrote about the cruelty of whites toward the native peoples of Australia. He once observed that "it is a most lamentable thing to think that the progress and prosperity of one race should conduce to the downfall and decay of another."

the trinkets Cook had brought along. Game was plentiful and hunting grounds ample, so there was no need for them to farm or fight tribal wars. Cook recorded his impressions: "They [the aborigines] live in a tranquillity which is not disturbed by the inequality of condition: the earth and the sea of their own accord furnish them with all things necessary for life ... they live in a warm and fine climate and enjoy a very wholesome air so that they have very little need of clothing ... they seem to set no value upon anything we gave them, nor would they ever part with anything of their own...." During their stay in Australia, Cook and his men also saw animals such as the kangaroo, flying fox, and dingo for the first time.

Once the *Endeavour* was repaired, Cook found a passage through the reef to the open sea. On the voyage back to England he was able to confirm that there was a strait between Australia and New Guinea. The *Endeavour* reached England on July 12, 1771, not quite three years after leaving.

Crosses Antarctic Circle

Although Cook's previous voyage seemed to show there was no large southern continent, this fact had not yet been conclusively proven. Cook therefore prepared another expedition in 1771. Now a commander in the Royal Navy, Cook requested that the Admiralty give him two new ships in case he encountered problems with one of the vessels on the voyage. Since the *Endeavour* was no longer seaworthy, two Whitby colliers were refitted and named the *Resolution* and the *Adventure*.

In mid-January 1773 Cook's ships crossed the Antarctic Circle, becoming the first vessels to accomplish this feat. In Antarctica, Cook and his crew found a dazzlingly white world, consisting of extreme cold, ice, and snow that almost had a will of its own. The crew's encounters with icebergs were intimidating and unnerving, as navigating through deep, narrow channels was close to impossible in ships propelled by wind power. Cook noticed that icebergs could be "as high as the dome of St. Pauls [a cathedral in London]," but they could be fragile, too, easily breaking up in the water and causing great danger to wooden ships.

Because the climate and conditions are so severe, it was possible to circumnavigate Antarctica only in the summer months. Cook made two unsuccessful attempts to sail around the continent. Before undertaking his third effort in 1774, he set aside nine months for his crew to recuperate. Cook also had to recover from an acute gallbladder attack that almost killed him.

Cook circumnavigates Antarctica

Sailing from New Zealand on November 10, 1774, Cook explored Tierra del Fuego, South Georgia, and the Sandwich Islands. After claiming South Georgia and the Sandwich Islands—both of which he found bleak and desolate—for Britain, Cook completed his circumnavigation of the South Pole on March 21, 1775. During his time in Antarctica Cook discovered a world populated by whales, seals, sea lions, penguins, geese, and seabirds. Cook wrote in his diary: "It is wonderful to see how the different animals which inhabit this little spot are reconciled to each other; they seem to have entered into a league not to disturb each other's tranquility." Yet Cook's own

ANTARCTIC SEA LIFE ANNIHILATED Within fifty years of Cook's trip to Antarctica, the sea life in the area had been wiped out by hunters from England, France, and America who were sent to kill the animals for profit. The number of animals that were slaughtered is hard to determine, but it is certain the total reached into the millions. The killings were brutal. For instance, friendly seals were hit on the backs of their heads with nail-studded clubs. During one season alone, sixty men on two ships killed forty-five thousand seals. By the 1830s, seals were virtually extinct in Antarctica. Then hunters turned their attention to killing whales for oil used in making candles. Again, the slaughter was indiscriminate, as pregnant mothers were massacred along with males. After hunters had killed all the whales in the breeding and mating grounds, ships hunted whales down in the open seas. Male whales would try to protect calves or females, with little success. Each season, countries would dispatch hundreds of ships in a highly competitive business that reaped huge profits until there were no more whales to kill. The annihilation of such a significant part of natural life, like the slaughter of the American buffalo on the prairies in the United States, is one of the more troubling stories in modern exploration.

crew set in motion the ultimate destruction of life in the Antarctic when they began indiscriminately killing sea lions on Staten Island for oil.

Cook tries to find Northwest Passage

Cook returned to England in 1775. The most remarkable aspect of the trip back from Antarctica was that, due to Cook's precautions, not a single person on his ship died of scurvy (a disease caused by lack of vitamin C). As a result of this accomplishment, Cook was elected to the Royal Society, which presented him with its gold medal. King George III also promoted him to captain.

In 1776 the British Admiralty decided that the answer to finding the long-sought Northwest Passage around North America was to approach the problem from the opposite direction—to look for it from the Pacific side. Although in poor health, Cook volunteered for the assignment. The *Resolution* was refitted, and a new Whitby collier was commissioned as the *Discovery,* to be commanded by Captain Charles Clerke. Cook sailed from England on the *Resolution* on July 12, 1776.

Discovers Hawaiian Islands

From Tahiti, Cook headed north toward Alaska, where he was to investigate possible routes east. Along the way, he found Christmas Island on December 25, 1777, and then made one of his most significant discoveries on January 18, 1778—the Hawaiian Islands, which he named the Sandwich Islands in honor of his patron, the Earl of Sandwich (full name, John Montagu; 1718–1792). Cook did not linger in Hawaii but continued his way northward. Once in Alaska, he tried various routes to see if they were connected with a passageway around America. Finding none, he decided to return to Hawaii. On the morning of January 17, 1779, Cook stepped ashore at Kealakeua Bay on the west coast of the "Big Island" of Hawaii. About fifteen hundred canoes had surrounded the two ships as the islanders came out to welcome Cook. The natives thought he was the reincarnation of Lono, the god of harvests and happiness. Cook was unaware of this, but he treated the ceremony with the same solemnity and dignity as the Hawaiians.

Hawaiians accept Cook as a god

Cook stayed on Hawaii for about three weeks. When he announced his departure his hosts were relieved. The presence of the foreigners, especially since they were gods and could be denied nothing, had been a strain on the Hawaiians. Two days after they departed, the two English ships ran into a storm, damaging one of the masts (an upright pole) of the *Resolution* and forcing a return to Hawaii for repairs. This time the Hawaiians were not happy to see the Europeans. When one of the sailors died, he was buried on shore, and the islanders learned that the Europeans were mortal. On February 13, a confrontation on the shore broke out over the theft of some of the Europeans' possessions and a Hawaiian chief was injured in the ensuing fight.

Cook killed

During the night, the small sailboat attached to the *Discovery* was stolen. The next morning, Cook went ashore, escorted by ten marines, to announce that he intended to take the local chief hostage until the boat was returned. A crowd of Hawaiians gathered to protect the chief. Then, realizing one of their canoes had

JAMES COOK James Cook was born on October 27, 1728, in the village of Marton, near Whitby in northern England. He received some education in the village school, but left at an early age. Apprenticed to a Whitby coal ship owner, Cook spent his spare time studying mathematics and navigation. (An apprentice agrees to work for a tradesman for a specific length of time in order to learn a skill.) After completing his apprenticeship, Cook sailed on various ships and in 1752 began working as a ship's mate. Cook joined the Royal Navy as an ordinary sailor—abandoning the chance to be the captain of a collier, or coal ship— to help his country in its fight against France in North America. Rising to the rank of warrant officer in 1757, Cook used his exceptional skills as a navigator and surveyor to map the coast of eastern Canada. Cook's fame comes from three expeditions he led to the Pacific and the ships he commanded: the *Endeavour,* the *Resolution,* the *Adventure,* and the *Discovery.*

been fired on from the ships, they began to throw stones. Cook decided he had to retreat. While he tried to make his way back down the beach to his boat, a group of British sailors on shore fired warning shots. Within seconds another group offshore began shooting. As Cook was turning to tell his men to cease fire, he stumbled and the Hawaiian mob fell upon him. Stabbing and clubbing him to death, the Hawaiians took Cook's dismembered body back to their village. After a few days they returned his remains to the British. The sailors then buried their captain in the bay. Following Cook's death, the *Resolution* and *Discovery* sailed north to the Kamchatka Peninsula and the coast of Siberia. Failing to find the Northwest Passage, the British sailed for home and reached England in October 1780.

FOR FURTHER REFERENCE

Books

Morehead, Alan. *Fatal Impact.* New York City: Harper & Row, 1988.

Mungo Park's Second Trip to the Niger River

1806

Mungo Park made several serious miscalculations that led to the devastating outcome of his second expedition.

Mungo Park was a Scottish doctor and the first European to see the Niger River in Africa and return to tell about it. Park made two expeditions to the African continent, both of which were beset with mishaps. When he returned to England from his first trip, Park wrote a best-selling book about the expedition. After settling back into his medical practice, however, he became bored and accepted an opportunity to explore the Niger once again. During the second expedition, Park remained resilient through one mishap after another, weathering the most adverse circumstances with grace and optimism. Eventually, however, Park's miscalculations led to his death in the river that brought him fame.

Chosen to explore the Niger

In 1788 famous British scientist Joseph Banks (1743–1820) founded the Association for Promoting the Discovery of the Interior Parts of Africa in London. At its first meeting the association decided that its major priority would be the discovery of the Niger River and the fabled city of Timbuktu. Europeans knew about both of these places from stories they had heard at trading posts on the west coast of Africa. No Westerner, however, had ever actually seen either the river or city. The association sent out two British explorers, Simon

Scottish doctor Mungo Park was the first European to see the Niger River in Africa.

Lucas and John Ledyard (1751–1789), but both men died within a short time of their arrival in North Africa.

In 1791 Irish explorer Daniel Houghton (1740–1791) was left to die while he was searching for the source of the Niger by Muslim tribesmen in what is now eastern Senegal. (Muslims are followers of Islam.) On Banks's recommendation, Park was selected to make the next attempt. Park intended to leave immediately for the Gambia River on the west coast of Africa in the company of the new British consul (an official who represents commercial interests). The official kept delaying his departure so long that Park finally set out on his own in May 1795, reaching Pisania, a town on the Gambia, in June. After spending time in Pisania learning Mandingo (the local language), Park departed at the beginning of December 1795, accompanied by a guide, a servant, and four porters.

Plagued by danger and misfortune

No sooner had Park embarked on his journey than he began to experience a series of misfortunes, some of them life-threatening. When he traveled northeast into Medina, the capital of the Kingdom of Woolli, he was well received by the king. Yet the king of neighboring Boxidou was suspicious of the British explorer, and Park was able to appease him only by giving him an umbrella. As a Christian, Park encountered outright hostility when he entered regions where Islam was the predominant religion. After Park reached the town of Benown he was imprisoned by the local king, Ali, for a month in a mud hut. When Ali and his men were attacked by rival tribes, they left town, taking Park with them. Along the way, the explorer was subjected to more mistreatment when his captors would not give him water and forced him to drink out of a cattle trough.

At the end of June, Park was finally able to escape on his horse in a crowd of refugees who were fleeing the fighting. His troubles, however, were not over. A gang of robbers took Park's cloak, which contained his money, so he had to resort to begging in order to survive. On several occasions Park nearly perished from thirst. Once he was saved by a rain squall (a sudden storm) when he was able to drink the water that he squeezed out of his clothes. Eventually he reached Bambara country, where the native population was friendlier. As he approached the capital of Segou, Park saw "with infinite pleasure the great object of my mission—the ... majestic Niger, glittering to the morning sun, as broad as the Thames [a river that flows through London] at Westminster [a district in London], and flowing slowly *to the eastward.*" After months of overcoming hazards and hardship, Park had finally found one of the great missing links in European knowledge of Africa.

Forced to return to England

Jubilant at his success, Park set out to explore the region around the Niger. He continued down the river, visiting the magnificent city of Segou, where the king gave Park cowrie shells for trading. (Cowrie shells are brightly colored seashells that local tribes used as money.) Park also planned to go on to Timbuktu (or Tombouctou), the mysterious city in present-day Mali. By July, however, he was sick and completely out of resources. At this point Park decided to return to the coast and take a ship back to England. He reached Bamako, the capital of Mali, the following month. Near Bamako thieves took most of his clothing, leaving him only a shirt and a pair of trousers. Fortunately Park managed to keep his hat, in which he had stuffed the notes he was writing about his journey. Park's religious faith reportedly prevented him from lapsing into despair, and he wrote that he was "assured that relief was at hand."

In September, Park met a slave trader named Kafra who agreed (for a price to be paid on arrival) to take the explorer along with a group of thirty-five slaves to the coast. The travelers had to wait at the town of Kamalia until the end of the rainy season, however, and did not start out until April. The march was horrific. The slaves were tied to one another with ropes around their necks, and their feet were fettered to keep them from running away. During the trip two of the women slaves committed suicide by eating clay. When the party finally reached Pisania, Park paid Kafra with a piece of cloth. His fortune improved considerably when he was able to find a position as the ship doctor on an American slave ship headed for the Caribbean. During the crossing he witnessed further horrors as 11 of the 130 slaves died.

Attempts to settle down

In Antigua (an island in the West Indies), Park took a ship bound for London. He arrived on December 25, 1797. No one in England even knew that Park was still alive. Since he did not want to disturb anyone on Christmas morning, he wandered the empty streets of the city. When he came to the gardens of the British Museum he noticed a gate was open. Stepping inside, he coincidentally stumbled upon James Dickson, his brother-in-law, who was doing some gardening chores. Park was warmly received in London. He later wrote a book about his African adventures that became a best-seller. In the summer of 1799 Park returned to Scotland and started a medical practice in the small town of Peebles. He also married the daughter of one of his college professors. Troubled by recurring illnesses from his trip to the Niger, Park suffered from nightmares about being captured and tortured.

Makes serious miscalculations

Still, Park had become bored. When he was offered the chance to lead another expedition to the Niger River, he accepted it immediately. Park was given temporary rank of lieutenant in the British Army and put in charge of a force of

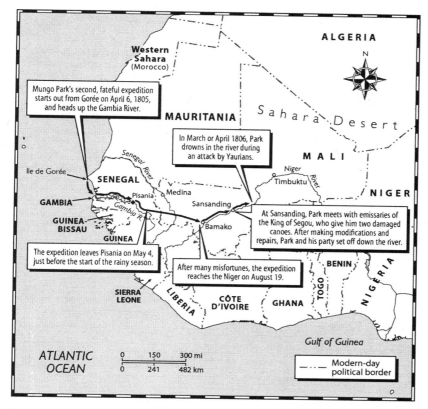

Mungo Park's second, fateful expedition starts out from Gorée on April 6, 1805, and heads up the Gambia River.

In March or April 1806, Park drowns in the river during an attack by Yaurians.

The expedition leaves Pisania on May 4, just before the start of the rainy season.

At Sansanding, Park meets with emissaries of the King of Segou, who give him two damaged canoes. After making modifications and repairs, Park and his party set off down the river.

After many misfortunes, the expedition reaches the Niger on August 19.

ALGERIA

Western Sahara (Morocco)

MAURITANIA

Sahara Desert

MALI

NIGER

Niger River
Timbuktu

Ile de Gorée
SENEGAL
Senegal River
Pisania   Medina
GAMBIA
Sansanding
Gambia R.
GUINEA-BISSAU
Bamako
GUINEA

BENIN

SIERRA LEONE

LIBERIA

CÔTE D'IVOIRE

GHANA

TOGO

NIGERIA

Gulf of Guinea

ATLANTIC OCEAN

| 0 | 150 | 300 mi |
| 0 | 241 | 482 km |

Modern-day political border

Before leaving on his second Niger River expedition, Mungo Park made several miscalculations that turned the trip into a nightmare.

about forty Europeans. Among the group were thirty soldiers from a British garrison in Gorée, an island off the coast of Senegal, where the expedition would begin. Park also hired a Mandingo guide named Isaaco and a few African servants. Before setting out he optimistically wrote, "I have little doubt that I shall be able, with presents and fair words, to pass through the country to Niger and if once we are fairly afloat, the day is won."

Park then made several serious miscalculations. First, he thought his men would be able to do all the heavy work of handling the pack animals. Then he assumed they would show the same exceptional resilience in meeting the hazards and discomforts of African travel that he had demonstrated on his previous expedition. An even more serious mistake was leaving at the worst time of the year, when the dry season was coming to an end.

The expedition set out from Goree on April 6, sailing up the Gambia River for Kayee. Three weeks later the party set out from Kayee on the overland journey to the Niger. The first day of the trip was horrible—the donkeys, laden with heavy loads, sat down and refused to budge. Some kicked and bucked to free themselves from their burden. Many of the soldiers, already exhausted, stole away to rest. On the second day, when the party arrived at Pisania, they stopped to reorganize. The expedition set out again from Pisania on May 4, just before the start of the rainy season. After three weeks of travel, during which the men covered two hundred miles, Park believed they were halfway to the Niger. He wrote to his wife of the group's good health and the welcome they had received from the natives.

The journey, however, was not at all as pleasant as Park would lead his wife to believe. Two soldiers had gotten sick with dysentery (a tropical disease), and one person had an epileptic fit. The group's guide, Isaaco, had been captured by local tribesmen and was released only after a show of force by the Europeans. Three days earlier Park's camp had been attacked by a swarm of bees and seven of the pack animals had been lost.

A multitude of mishaps

Park's luck would not turn. A week later the first storm broke over the travelers, and the rain did not stop. Still the party continued. Throughout the next weeks, they were bombarded with misfortune. Soldiers were too ill to walk and were mounted on animals. The natives were not always friendly and the country was full of dangerous animals. Several dying men had to be left behind, and a soldier drowned while crossing a river. Isaaco was attacked by a crocodile and was finally freed after his leg was badly mauled. Then Park's men were chased by two tornadoes. By the end of the July, when the death toll had risen to twenty, all the expedition's pack animals had been lost or stolen. The men managed to replace the animals, however, and continued their perilous trek. At last, on August 19, the party saw the Niger. Park wrote, "The sight of the river promised at least an alleviation on our toils." Although he reflected with gloom on what had been lost, he still convinced himself that all would turn out well in the end.

Recovering briefly from these disasters, Park and the other survivors struggled into Bamako on the Niger. They hired canoes

MUNGO PARK Mungo Park was born in the village of Foulshiels near the town of Selkirk in Scotland on September 10, 1771. He was the tenth of thirteen children born to a farmer and his wife. Park took courses in anatomy and surgery at the University of Edinburgh but never graduated. Leaving school, he went to London, England, where he stayed with a sister and her husband. Park's brother-in-law was acquainted with famous scientist Joseph Banks, who gave Park a job as a ship's doctor on a trading vessel. Park impressed Banks, who nominated him to be the next explorer sent out to find the Niger. After this first voyage, Park went back to Scotland where he married the daughter of one of his college professors. The couple had three sons, yet Park soon tired of a settled life. Telling a friend he would "rather brave Africa and all its horrors, than wear out his life in long and toilsome rides over the hills of Scotland," he accepted the chance to lead a second expedition to Africa.

to carry the rest of the expedition downstream. Park became ill with dysentery himself. At Sansanding, he was met by emissaries (representatives) of the King of Segou. Park told the men he planned to sail down the Niger to the sea. If he found the way, he would open up direct trade relations with the Africans, bypassing Arab middlemen. Park brought out presents that included a silver-plated tureen (a large bowl), a pair of silver-mounted, double-barreled guns, a sabre (a long sword) in a morocco leather case, and bales of cloth. Park offered these items for the king in return for protection in all his dominions. The emissaries granted Park's request, giving him two damaged canoes in exchange. After working eighteen days Park's men repaired the canoes and joined them together. Park christened the new vessel His Majesty's Schooner *Joliba* (the African name for the Niger). Just before he embarked Park wrote what would be his last letter home, assuring his wife that everything was fine. Isaaco took the letter, along with messages from other members of the party, back up the coast on November 19, 1805. In Isaaco's place was a new guide named Ahmadi Fatouma.

Died fighting on Niger

Park's letter offered the last words ever heard from the explorer. Five years later, the British government hired Isaaco to go into the African interior to try to find out what had happened to Park's party. In Sansanding, Isaaco met Fatouma and got the story. Park and his men had proceeded down the river, using their firearms to force their way rather than negotiating passage with the local rulers. When Park sent Fatouma to try to present gifts to the king of the small Hausa state of Yauri, about six hundred miles from the Gulf of Guinea, the king found the gifts inadequate. The next morning the Yaurians attacked Park and his men. Realizing they would not prevail, Park and the soldiers jumped into the river and were drowned. Only one slave survived and made it to Yauri to tell the story to Fatouma.

Although there are discrepancies in Fatouma's story, it is the only reliable account anyone has been able to piece together. Nevertheless, many people refused to believe that a man who had successfully surmounted so many great dangers and survived a multitude of misadventures could be dead. In fact, at the time of her death in 1840, Park's wife still believed her husband was alive somewhere in Africa. One of the couple's three sons, Thomas—a midshipman in the Royal Navy—was given three years' leave in 1827 to search for his father. Thomas died of fever on his way into the interior of Africa. Park's almanac, which was once lost, was found in 1857 and now resides in the museum of the Royal Geographical Society in London.

FOR FURTHER REFERENCE

Books

McLynn, Frank. *Hearts of Darkness: The European Exploration of Africa.* New York City: Carroll & Graf, 1992.

Peter Skene Ogden and the Columbia River Territory

1824 TO 1830

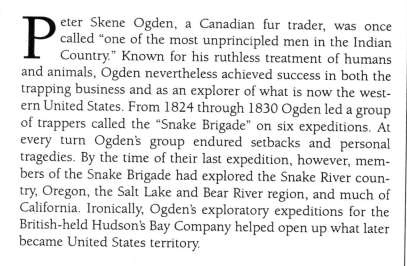

P eter Skene Ogden, a Canadian fur trader, was once called "one of the most unprincipled men in the Indian Country." Known for his ruthless treatment of humans and animals, Ogden nevertheless achieved success in both the trapping business and as an explorer of what is now the western United States. From 1824 through 1830 Ogden led a group of trappers called the "Snake Brigade" on six expeditions. At every turn Ogden's group endured setbacks and personal tragedies. By the time of their last expedition, however, members of the Snake Brigade had explored the Snake River country, Oregon, the Salt Lake and Bear River region, and much of California. Ironically, Ogden's exploratory expeditions for the British-held Hudson's Bay Company helped open up what later became United States territory.

Gains reputation for ruthlessness

In the early nineteenth century a bitter competition for the fur trade raged between two British companies in North America: Hudson's Bay Company (HBC), which was controlled from London, England, and North West Company, which was based in Montreal, Canada. Ogden was employed by the North West Company. He quickly gained a reputation for being one of the most violent and ruthless of all the traders. He was

Ironically, Ogden's exploratory expeditions for the British-held Hudson's Bay Company helped open up what later became United States territory.

PETER SKENE OGDEN Peter Skene Ogden (1790–1854) was born in Quebec City, Canada. His father was a native of the United States who left the country during the American Revolution (1775–83) because he supported the British king, George III. When Ogden was four years old, his father was appointed to a judgeship in Montreal, Quebec, and the family relocated. Montreal was the center of the fur trade in North America at that time, and many young men were drawn to the city in hopes of making their fortune. Instead of following in his father's footsteps into the legal profession like his brothers, Ogden entered the fur trade as an employee of the North West Company in 1809.

accused of a number of crimes in Canada, including the 1818 murder of a Native American who traded with North West's rival, the HBC. In order to put Ogden out of reach of the law, the North West Company sent him to its most remote posts in what is now the Pacific Northwest of the United States.

Unfortunately for Ogden, the two rival fur companies decided their competition was only helping their American rivals, and in 1821 they decided to unite under the name "Hudson's Bay Company" (still HBC). Ogden was so hated by the directors of the HBC that one of the provisions of the agreement was that he was not to be employed by the joint company. At about this time, the HBC sent out company official George Simpson (1792–1860), who took charge of posts in what are now Oregon, Washington, Idaho, and British Columbia. This area was claimed by both Great Britain and the United States, a territory dispute would not be settled until 1846. Simpson felt that if Britain were to prevail against its rival, it would have to make use of its most ruthless men, including Ogden. Under Simpson's influence, the HBC agreed to rehire Ogden. In 1824 Ogden was instructed to travel to the Snake River country in present-day Idaho.

Has conflict with American trappers

At first Ogden had amicable relations with American trappers. On December 20, 1824, he left Flathead House at Flathead Lake in northern Montana with a party of fifty-eight people, including engagées (people hired to help) and their wives and children. Ogden met up with the famous American trapper

Jedediah Smith (1799–1831) near present-day Missoula, Montana. For the next two months the men joined forces, trapping as far south as the Bear River in southeastern Idaho. Smith's party then departed for other territory. As Ogden and his men traveled onward, one of his trappers, Thomas McKay, climbed a high mountain and saw far to the west "a large lake which Bear River falls into." This was the first recorded sighting of the Great Salt Lake, although Americans were known to have seen it previously. Ogden also learned that the Bear River had nothing to do with the Spanish River, indicating his Canadian brigade was the first group to go far enough south along the Bear River to determine that it flows into the Salt Lake. The triumph of this discovery was to be tragically overshadowed, however, by a disaster that would soon strike the expedition.

Hostilities soon began to develop between Ogden and rival trappers. On May 23, 1825, John Gardner and a party of freelance American trappers invaded Ogden's campsite at Mountain Green, east of Salt Lake. Gardner's party raised an American flag, claiming Ogden and his men were trespassing (in actuality, the territory belonged to Mexico). Ogden's expedition then disbanded and many of his trappers deserted to the American camp. Gardner's final blow was to steal furs and whatever else his men could find from Ogden's group. A devastated Ogden wrote in his journal on the night of May 26: "Here I am, surrounded on all sides by enemies and our expectations and hopes blasted for returns this year."

Having no other alternative, Ogden turned north to Walla Walla, Washington, arriving on November 2, 1825. By this time, he had seen more of the West in one season that any other trader. Ogden's travels had made it possible for mapmaker William Kittson to trace that part of the country on a manuscript map. Kittson's representation of the area is perhaps the best documentation now available about the fur traders' knowledge of the mountain West at that time. Ironically, since Kittson was working for the Americans, the map made possible the later expansion of the United States into territory that Ogden was exploring for Britain.

Encounters hardship

In the late winter and early spring of 1826 Ogden trapped in the Snake River country as far east as the Portneuf River in

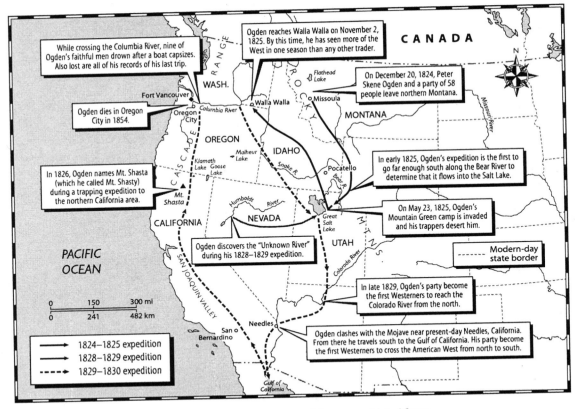

Peter Skene Ogden and his "Snake Brigade" explored large areas of the western United States.

Text within the map image:

While crossing the Columbia River, nine of Ogden's faithful men drown after a boat capsizes. Also lost are all of his records of his last trip.

Ogden reaches Walla Walla on November 2, 1825. By this time, he has seen more of the West in one season than any other trader.

CANADA

On December 20, 1824, Peter Skene Ogden and a party of 58 people leave northern Montana.

Ogden dies in Oregon City in 1854.

In 1826, Ogden names Mt. Shasta (which he called Mt. Shasty) during a trapping expedition to the northern California area.

In early 1825, Ogden's expedition is the first to go far enough south along the Bear River to determine that it flows into the Salt Lake.

On May 23, 1825, Ogden's Mountain Green camp is invaded and his trappers desert him.

Ogden discovers the "Unknown River" during his 1828–1829 expedition.

PACIFIC OCEAN

Modern-day state border

In late 1829, Ogden's party become the first Westerners to reach the Colorado River from the north.

Ogden clashes with the Mojave near present-day Needles, California. From there he travels south to the Gulf of California. His party become the first Westerners to cross the American West from north to south.

1824–1825 expedition
1828–1829 expedition
1829–1830 expedition

eastern Idaho near present-day Pocatello. He then returned to Walla Walla. In September 1826, after only two months' rest, he headed out again. This time he went south through eastern Oregon to Malheur Lake and Klamath Lake in northern California. Before turning back north Ogden saw and named Mount Shasta (which he called "Mt. Shasty"), the tallest peak in the Cascade Range. In spite of his successes, however, Ogden encountered numerous hardships. In the region around Goose Lake on the California-Oregon border, for instance, the only thing available to drink was liquid mud. Ogden wrote in his journal that "this is certainly a most horrid life."

In August 1827 Ogden was again leading a brigade east to the Snake River and the Portneuf of Idaho. Meeting a band of American trappers led by Samuel Tullock, Ogden was able take revenge for Gardner's attack at Mountain Green.

Inadvertently opens way for American settlement

The most significant of Ogden's expeditions took place the following season, 1828–29. In addition to discovering the Humboldt River, which Ogden called the "Unknown River," he recorded his first view of the Great Salt Lake. Although he was not aware of it at the time, Ogden had found one of the great links in the immigrant road, the Oregon Trail. The trail would take Ogden's rivals, the Americans, on to the Pacific and California, and would ultimately lead to the British loss of the Columbia River territory.

Fights Native Americans, crosses Western frontier

Ogden's widest-ranging expedition was his last, and perhaps one of his most harrowing. Leaving the Columbia River in October 1829, Ogden went south to the Humboldt Sink and had a clash with local Native Americans. He then turned south until he reached the Colorado River, probably becoming the first Westerner to approach the river from the north. During the journey Ogden marched his men across the desert, forcing them to eat their dying horses for food and drink the animals' blood to keep from perishing of thirst. The party also met a Mojave tribe near present-day Needles, California. Ogden's encounter with the Mojave ended well for the Snake Brigade. When the Indians charged his party, Ogden ordered his men to fire a volley into them, followed by a charge with homemade spears. "The first, however, sufficed," Ogden recalled, "for on seeing the number of their fellows who in a single moment were made to lick the dust, the rest ingloriously fled, and we saw no more of them." From this point, Ogden and his party followed the Colorado River south all the way to the Gulf of California. The men were the first Westerners to cross the American West from north to south.

Records lost in tragic mishap

Heading back north, Ogden led his men through Cajon Pass near San Bernardino, California, and then into San Joaquin Valley. Avoiding the Mexican mission stations, Ogden made it to northern California and then took his previous trail north from Klamath Lake. While the party was crossing the

"FIFTY-FOUR FORTY OR FIGHT" During the late eighteenth century Russian and British fur trappers and traders moved into the Pacific Northwest. Soon the coast of present-day Oregon became an important link in international commerce, as ships from many nations came to trade furs with Native Americans. By the turn of the nineteenth century a rivalry had developed between the British and the United States over claims to the area around the Columbia River. In 1818, when Peter Skene Ogden was beginning his career with the North West Company, a treaty gave the United States and Great Britain joint rights in Oregon for ten years. The treaty was later extended. Within twenty-five years American wagon trains had begun what was known as the "Great Migration" west over the Oregon Trail.

Soon these settlers were having conflicts with the British. Moving to form their own government, the Americans demanded that the British get out of the Columbia River country up to latitude fifty-four degrees, forty north. During the 1844 United States presidential election, a popular slogan was "Fifty-four forty or fight." War with Britain was prevented in 1846 when the latitude was set at forty-nine degrees north. Two years later the Oregon Territory was created, expanding American possession to the entire area west of the Rocky Mountains, between the forty-second and forty-ninth parallels.

Columbia River, tragedy struck. One of the expedition's boats capsized, drowning nine of Ogden's men. Also lost were all of Ogden's records of the trip.

Expands British claims, named HBC director

In 1830 Ogden established an HBC post at the mouth of the Nass River, near what is now the southern border of Alaska. At the Nass River post, he fought off competition from the Americans and the Russians. Ogden was made the director of all of mainland British Columbia for the HBC in 1834. In 1844 Ogden went to England for a year, then he returned to the Pacific Northwest with a secret British surveying team that was tracing a route from eastern Canada to the Columbia River. At the time, Britain and the United States were engaged in a dispute—which briefly threatened to turn into a war—over what would later become the Oregon Territory. British efforts to retain their joint claims with the United States ended in 1846 when the boundary settlement extended the forty-ninth parallel boundary all the way to the Pacific Ocean, giving present-day Washington and Oregon to the United States.

Ogden remained with the HBC in what was now American territory. In late 1847 he led a team that negotiated the release of American prisoners taken by members of the Cayuse tribe, who had attacked a mission station near Walla Walla. Ogden spent his final years at Fort Vancouver, Washington. After becoming ill in 1854, he went to Oregon City to seek medical help. Ogden died shortly thereafter.

Achievements eclipsed by 1846 agreement

Ogden was one of the great explorers of the American West. A colorful, tenacious figure, he unrelentingly confronted the frontier to chart unknown territory. Almost as important as his exploits were the reports and the maps he submitted to the HBC office in London. Ogden's knowledge was later passed on to world-famous cartographers (map makers) Aaron Arrowsmith and Sons and A.H. Brué of Paris, France. Along with data collected by American explorers such as Meriweather Lewis (1774–1809), William Clark (1770–1838), and David Thompson (1770–1857), Ogden's information formed the basis of commercial maps used for several decades. His explorations were instrumental in determining the boundaries of what would become the United States. Yet this outcome negated the primary purpose of Ogden's missions, which was to claim as much land as possible for British commercial interests on the Western frontier. To a great extent, therefore, Ogden's exploring achievements had been in vain.

FOR FURTHER REFERENCE

Books

Goetzmann, William H. *Exploration and Empire.* New York City: Knopf, 1966.

The Donner Party Tragedy

APRIL 1846 TO APRIL 1847

One of the most memorable tragedies in the history of American western migration is the story of the Donner Party. Led by George and Jacob Donner, this group of eighty-one people was bound for the Sacramento Valley of California when they became stranded by snow while trying to cross the Sierra Nevada near the California-Nevada border. The Donner brothers' fatal decision to try a new short-cut cost the travelers precious time. When the party arrived at a crucial pass through the mountains, the snow was too deep for their wagons. Lacking food and adequate shelter, about half of the group died during the winter of 1846–47. Some members of the party resorted to eating the bodies of the dead in order to survive.

In April 1846 brothers George and Jacob Donner loaded their families into six wagons for a move from Illinois to California. James Reed and his family decided to join the Donner group for the journey west. At the time the party left Illinois, leaders George and Jacob Donner were both prosperous farmers in their sixties. Unfortunately, neither brother had any mountaineering or frontier skills. As a result, they made some poor decisions on the trip that resulted in death and disaster.

The Donner Party was bound for the Sacramento Valley of California when they became stranded by snow while trying to cross the Sierra Nevada.

Westward on the Oregon-California Trail

The Oregon-California Trail (a route west from Missouri to California and Oregon) was still new in 1846. Although more and more migrants were using the 2,000-mile route, the trail itself was often poorly marked. There were few guides and almost no published information for travelers to rely on. The members of the Donner Party had little experience or know-how to help them survive the hardships they would encounter on their way west.

The Donner-Reed wagons crossed into Wyoming in July 1846. In Wyoming the pioneers heard about a shortcut called the "Hastings Cutoff." The man promoting this shortcut, Lansford Hastings, had written a book called *The Emigrants' Guide to Oregon and California.* Hastings's book was one of the few guides for travelers on the trail. The author claimed his shortcut saved 400 miles for travelers by taking them southwest through Utah to Nevada, cutting off a corner of the usual route. The Donners were intrigued by this idea.

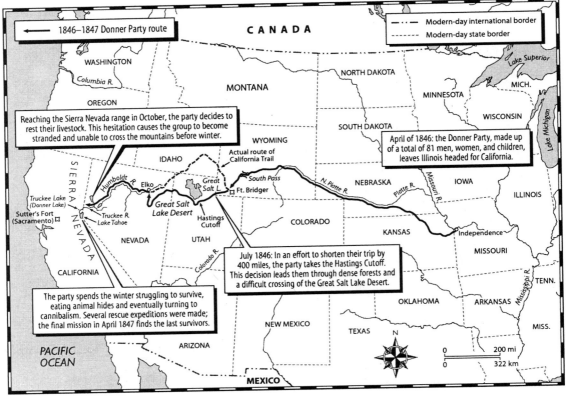

On their journey to California, the leaders of the Donner Party decided to take the Hastings Cutoff shortcut. This decision would eventually prove fatal for many members of the group.

Map labels:

1846–1847 Donner Party route

CANADA

Modern-day international border
Modern-day state border

WASHINGTON
Columbia R.
OREGON

MONTANA

NORTH DAKOTA
SOUTH DAKOTA

MINNESOTA
MICH.
Lake Superior
WISCONSIN
Lake Michigan

Reaching the Sierra Nevada range in October, the party decides to rest their livestock. This hesitation causes the group to become stranded and unable to cross the mountains before winter.

IDAHO
WYOMING
Actual route of California Trail

April of 1846: the Donner Party, made up of a total of 81 men, women, and children, leaves Illinois headed for California.

SIERRA NEVADA
Humboldt R.
Elko
Great Salt L.
South Pass
Ft. Bridger
N. Platte R.
NEBRASKA
IOWA
ILLINOIS

Truckee Lake (Donner Lake)
Sutter's Fort (Sacramento)
Truckee R.
Lake Tahoe
Great Salt Lake Desert
Hastings Cutoff
Platte R.
Missouri R.

NEVADA
UTAH
COLORADO
KANSAS
Independence
MISSOURI

July 1846: In an effort to shorten their trip by 400 miles, the party takes the Hastings Cutoff. This decision leads them through dense forests and a difficult crossing of the Great Salt Lake Desert.

CALIFORNIA
Colorado R.

The party spends the winter struggling to survive, eating animal hides and eventually turning to cannibalism. Several rescue expeditions were made; the final mission in April 1847 finds the last survivors.

NEW MEXICO
TEXAS
OKLAHOMA
ARKANSAS
Mississippi R.
TENN.
MISS.

PACIFIC OCEAN
ARIZONA

MEXICO

N

0   200 mi
0   322 km

Party splits off from the main trail

The Donner group made their first serious error at a place called the South Pass (an area in central Wyoming). On July 31, a sizable wagon train led by George Donner split off from the regular route to try the Hastings Cutoff shortcut. In addition to the Donners, there were six other families with the group, along with a few hired hands and domestic workers. Some of the women in the party argued that the main trail would be safer, but they were overruled. Nineteen wagons turned away from the main trail at Fort Bridger, Wyoming, that day.

This decision soon proved to be a terrible mistake. The pioneers faced great difficulties along the new route. For part of the journey they were forced to cut a passage for the wagons through dense woods. Later they had to cross the Great Salt Lake Desert, a dry region of northwestern Utah covering

4,000 square miles. In the desert, the party lost many of their pack animals. The harsh conditions took a toll on the human travelers as well. One member of the party, thirteen-year-old Virginia Reed, later described this part of the journey by writing, "It seemed as though the hand of death had been laid upon the country."

Another foolhardy decision

Exhausted and frightened, the party joined the main trail again near what is now Elko, Nevada, on September 30. It was very late in the year to be facing the mountain crossing that lay ahead. The wagons finally reached the eastern slopes of the Sierra Nevada in mid-October. There the group decided to rest their livestock for a week before starting over the mountains. With winter snows expected any day—which would make crossing impossible—this delay was another serious mistake. But the party and its leaders were not in the best condition to make decisions. Worn out and low on food, the group had lost its sense of unity. A knife fight had already resulted in one death, and the killer, James Reed, had been banished from the group. (Ironically, Reed reached California safely and was instrumental in getting help for the rest of the party.)

It was the end of October when most of the wagons reached the shores of Truckee Lake (now Donner Lake) in northern California. Looming above at 7,088 feet were the Sierra Nevada and the narrow, rocky passage now known as Donner Pass. (Donner Pass is located about thirty-five miles southwest of Reno, Nevada.) The eastern side of the mountains is steep, but if the pioneers had made it up through the pass, they could have proceeded down the easier slope of the western side to Sutter's Fort in the Great Central Valley of California in a few days. The Donner Party, however, did not get a chance to cross the mountains. Just a day's journey from the pass, at their temporary stop by the lake, the pioneers watched as heavy snow began to fall.

Snowbound pioneers struggle to survive

Three times the party tried to climb to the pass, but the wagons could not make it through the deep snow. There was no choice but to return to the lake and set up a camp for the

WHICH DONNER PARTY MEMBERS SURVIVED—AND WHY?

About half the Donner Party died during their winter ordeal. Among the Donners themselves, both George and Jacob died, along with their wives and four male children. But eight of the Donner children survived to be rescued—orphaned but alive. James Reed, who had been cast out of the group for knifing a man, was not at the camp with his wife and three children during the winter. Yet all of the Reed family survived, including James, his wife Margaret, and their three children. Patrick Breen (who wrote about the ordeal in his diary) and his wife Margaret both lived, and the couple was able to keep their seven children alive as well.

What made the difference for those who lived? Historians see clear patterns when they look at the individual members of the Donner Party. Women survived more often than men and, among those who died, women survived longer than men. Experts say this may have happened because most women are physically and biologically structured to withstand cold and starvation better than men. For example, women need less food to survive and their higher proportion of body fat provides both protection from the cold and a supply of calories in times of famine.

Another factor seems to have been the nature of the relationships between people in the group. People who were traveling without family (for example, hired hands or single men) died at twice the rate of those who traveled with their families. Finally, the oldest and youngest members of the party were more likely to die than members between the ages of six and thirty-five. Children between the ages of six and fourteen had the best chance for survival—only two out of twenty-one such children died.

---

winter. Meanwhile, the Donner brothers, whose wagons had fallen behind the main party, also set up camp at nearby Alder Creek. The members of both groups faced spending the bitterly cold winter sheltered only by tents and makeshift cabins. Walking back and forth between the two camps, the travelers remained in contact with each other as often as winter conditions permitted.

The weather made each day a struggle for survival. Snow drifted as high as twenty feet. The lake was frozen. Food supplies were soon gone, and hunting generally failed to provide any food. Eventually, those who had not already died began to eat boiled animal hides. Patrick Breen, whose family was locked in beside the lake, described the situation on January 17 in his diary: "Provisions [food and supplies] scarce, hides are the only article we depend on, we have a little meat yet, may God send us help." Finally, in desperation, some of those who had not yet died of hunger or cold resorted to eating the bodies of their dead fellow travelers.

Help too late for many

In a desperate attempt to get help, fifteen of the strongest survivors set out on foot for Sutter's Fort. The group consisted of five women and ten men, including two Native American guides. Lost, cold, and starving, members of this party eventually killed and ate the Native Americans. Finally, the five women and two of the men arrived at a ranch forty miles from Sutter's Fort. It was not until mid-February that winter conditions subsided enough to enable rescuers to cross the mountains and bring help to the survivors of the Donner Party. Four rescue expeditions were made to Donner Lake that spring. The last mission, which reached the camps in April, found only one living person, a man named Lewis Keseberg. His only food for some time had been the corpse of George Donner's wife, Tamsen Donner.

Park and museum dedicated to Donner Party

The Donner Memorial State Park and Emigrant Trail Museum are located in Truckee, California, on the Overland Emigrant Trail. The Pioneer Monument on the site features a twenty-two-foot-tall stone pedestal that reaches the height of the snowdrifts that confronted the Donner Party. Each year visitors to the park and museum can participate in hikes over parts of the route taken by the Donner Party.

FOR FURTHER REFERENCE

Books

Lavender, David Sievert. *Snowbound: The Tragic Story of the Donner Party.* New York: Holiday House, 1996.

Murphy, Virginia Reed. *Across the Plains in the Donner Party.* North Haven, CT : Linnet Books, 1996.

Other

Overland Journeys to the Pacific. [Videocassette] Public Broadcasting Service (PBS-TV), 1992.

The Disappearance of John Franklin's Expedition

1847

For nearly a decade after Franklin's disappearance near Baffin Bay, Canada, the British government sponsored a series of search parties to try and locate the explorer and his crew.

The disappearance of British naval officer John Franklin's expedition triggered a long and complex search for the explorer and his men. Prior to vanishing in 1847, Franklin had led two other disastrous expeditions to the Canadian Arctic in search of the Northwest Passage (a ship route along the Arctic coast north of Canada to connect the Atlantic and Pacific Oceans). Franklin set out on his first journey, an overland exploration, in 1819. Due to harsh conditions and lack of food, the journey ended in disappointment. Franklin made his second unsuccessful attempt in 1825. Twenty years later he undertook his final, ill-fated trip with over one hundred men in two ships. Last seen in northern Baffin Bay, Canada, the party disappeared without a trace.

For nearly a decade, the British government sponsored a series of search parties for Franklin's expedition, with no success. One searcher, explorer Robert McClure, managed to find the Northwest Passage, but no evidence of Franklin's party. Finally, in 1854, news of the lost expedition came from an Inuit tribe near Baffin Bay. (The term "Inuit" refers to the Eskimo peoples of North America, especially Arctic Canada and Greenland.) Five years later the remains of the Franklin expedition were found during a search sponsored by Franklin's widow. Based on the evidence, the explorer and all of his men died in the Canadian wilderness without ever seeing the Northwest Passage.

First exploration a struggle to survive

Hoping to find a Northwest Passage over Canada, the British Admiralty sent Franklin and a small party to the Canadian Arctic in 1819. The men were to explore the north coast of Canada from the Coppermine River to Hudson Bay. Franklin's group landed in Manitoba and traveled overland with fur traders. They entered unknown territory north of the Great Slave Lake in the summer of 1820 and built a base camp, Fort Enterprise, on Winter Lake.

In July 1821 the men set out for the north coast with a party of trappers. Franklin soon discovered that the trappers were not very much help. The travelers had gone only a short distance along the coastline before winter set in, forcing everyone to return to Fort Enterprise. On the return trip half of the trappers died of starvation, and one killed a British officer. When the remaining men reached Fort Enterprise, they discovered that Native Americans had raided the fort and taken all of its supplies. Only by bartering with the Native Americans was Franklin's group able to survive the winter.

Prior to vanishing in 1847, John Franklin had led two other disastrous expeditions to the Canadian Arctic in search of a Northwest Passage.

Another failure, then disappearance

In spite of the failure of the expedition, Franklin was promoted to captain and welcomed as a hero when he returned to England. He began his second voyage to the Canadian north in 1825. This time he traveled to Great Bear Lake and built a supply fort on the western shore. His plan was to travel north up the Mackenzie River to the coast, then go west to Point Barrow, Alaska. Again Franklin's attempt failed. Forced to turn back after going about halfway, Franklin returned to England in 1827.

Franklin did not undertake another expedition for almost twenty years. Then, in 1845, he again set out for northern Canada. By this time he was fifty-eight years old, but he had high hopes for success because his two ships and one hundred and twenty-nine men had enough provisions to last three years. Soon, however, disaster struck. A few months after they had embarked from London, Franklin and his party were spotted by whalers in northern Baffin Bay, Canada. After this sighting, the men were never seen again. Franklin's expedition had disappeared without a trace.

Ross searches Arctic for Franklin

Because Franklin had been expected to spend some time in the Arctic, it was not until 1848 that the British Admiralty began to worry about his fate. Urged on by Jane Franklin, the explorer's wife, the government sent naval officer James Clark Ross (1800–1862) to look for him in May 1848. Ross was instructed to search in the area of Melville Sound, Banks Island, and the Wellington Channel. Ice, however, forced the party to stop at a point much farther east called Somerset Island. The Ross party was only seventy miles away from Franklin's first winter camp, but all efforts to find the missing men failed. Ross sent out sledges (sled-like vehicles with long runners) overland to search for the men. He also fired off guns and rockets and even released foxes wearing collars with messages engraved on them. But the searchers discovered nothing, and Ross returned to England with no news of the missing men.

McClure makes daring attempt

A principal figure in the next search was the Irish-born naval officer Robert McClure (1807–1873), who had served with Ross's expedition. In 1850 McClure was put in charge of the vessel *Investigator* under the general command of Captain Richard Collinson, who sailed on the *Enterprise*. McClure and Collinson hoped to solve the mystery of Franklin's disappearance by attacking the problem from the opposite side—the Pacific Ocean and Alaska, rather than the Atlantic. The expedition ships, however, were separated during the voyage by a storm in the Pacific. McClure guided the *Investigator* on a shortcut through the Aleutian Islands (a chain of islands that extends west from the Alaska Peninsula). He reached the Bering Strait between Alaska and Siberia before Collinson.

For unknown reasons, McClure did not wait for Collinson; instead, he set off on his own. McClure rammed the *Investigator* through patches of pack ice. Sometimes he used rowboats to tow the ship. Forced by the ice to travel east along the coast of Alaska, McClure finally managed to reach the south shore of Banks Island. To the east of this island McClure saw a channel (later named Prince of Wales Strait) with an open stretch of water leading northeast. As the *Investigator* sailed through, McClure realized that if this body of water connected with Melville Sound, he had found the long-sought Northwest Passage.

Discovery and near-disaster

By this time, however, winter was coming. At a point about thirty miles south of McClure's goal, Melville Sound, the *Investigator* was forced to stop by increasing ice and rising winds. Wind pushed the ship thirty miles back down the channel. The growing ice toppled the vessel over on its side, threatening to crush it against some rocks. McClure's men were convinced they were doomed. The storm died down, however, and the ship righted itself. Now, however, the *Investigator* was iced in for the winter.

Ship or no ship, McClure was determined to proceed north in search of a water passage. He took seven men and headed overland in sledges. After six days, the group climbed a small mountain and looked out on Melville Sound. McClure and his men had found the Northwest Passage, achieving a victory for the British. With the ship locked in ice for the winter, McClure now turned his attention back to Franklin. He sent out three land parties to search for traces of the expedition, without any success. During the following summer, McClure again attempted to navigate the passage he had found, but ice blocked his ship. McClure's party spent the winter of 1851–52 on the north coast of Banks Island. During the summer of 1852, the men tried unsuccessfully to free the ship from the ice. By September it became obvious they were going to have to spend another winter in the Arctic. Food supplies were dangerously low. Twenty of the men were ill from scurvy (a disease caused by a lack of vitamin C), and two officers were showing signs of insanity.

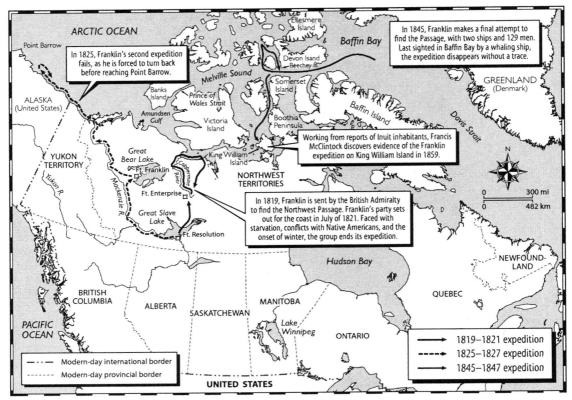

ARCTIC OCEAN

In 1845, Franklin makes a final attempt to find the Passage, with two ships and 129 men. Last sighted in Baffin Bay by a whaling ship, the expedition disappears without a trace.

In 1825, Franklin's second expedition fails, as he is forced to turn back before reaching Point Barrow.

Working from reports of Inuit inhabitants, Francis McClintock discovers evidence of the Franklin expedition on King William Island in 1859.

In 1819, Franklin is sent by the British Admiralty to find the Northwest Passage. Franklin's party sets out for the coast in July of 1821. Faced with starvation, conflicts with Native Americans, and the onset of winter, the group ends its expedition.

→	1819–1821 expedition
- ->	1825–1827 expedition
⊢⊢⊢>	1845–1847 expedition

--- Modern-day international border
---- Modern-day provincial border

John Franklin's three trips in search of a Northwest Passage all ended in disaster. On his last trip, Franklin—along with his entire crew—disappeared near Baffin Bay.

Meanwhile, Captain Henry Kellett, who had been sent to look for McClure and Collinson (who had also disappeared), arrived at Melville Island. Kellett found a note from McClure giving his position. Kellett's own ship was iced in, and he could not reach McClure until April 1853. Both Kellett's and McClure's men had to endure another winter in the Arctic. Due in part to McClure's refusal to abandon the *Investigator*, the ice trapped the group before they could escape during a brief thaw. The survivors finally returned to England on supply ships in late 1854.

John Ross organizes a private expedition

While McClure and Kellett were stranded in the Arctic, yet another well-known British explorer mounted an expedition to find Franklin. John Ross (1777–1856), an uncle of James Clark Ross, had taken great interest in the whereabouts of the

Franklin party. Unable to persuade the British government to sponsor his voyage, Ross organized a privately-funded expedition on a small ship called the *Zelix*. Ross and his crew spent the winter of 1850–51 in Barrow Strait. Unfortunately the party was too poorly equipped to help much in the search for Franklin. Like his nephew, Ross found no trace of the missing men.

Francis McClintock: four voyages in search of Franklin

The explorer who finally found the remains of the Franklin expedition was Francis Leopold McClintock (1819–1907). McClintock was involved in three futile search attempts, however, before completing a successful mission. McClintock had first served on James Clark Ross's ship during the initial search in 1848 and 1849. At that time McClintock had taken charge of sledge trips to the interior to try to find Franklin. He had come within 180 miles of the place where Franklin had died, but at a great cost to his men: all of them were sick when they returned to the ship. (The British did not believe in using dogs for sledge trips at that time, so they relied on men to pull the sledges.)

In 1850 McClintock was involved a search commanded by Horatio Austin. While the men's ship was anchored in Barrow Strait for the winter, McClintock had taken six sledge teams to explore the interior. No traces of Franklin's expedition were found, however, and the men returned to England in 1851. In the meantime, Jane Franklin had continued to campaign for the discovery of her husband's fate. Responding to her pleas in 1852, the British government sent out five ships under the command of Edward Belcher. McClintock was in charge of one of these ships, the *Intrepid*. On his third attempt to find Franklin, McClintock took charge of the sledge teams. He made an incredible 1,328-mile sledge trip during which another man died. Again McClintock met defeat when the *Intrepid* became hopelessly iced in and had to be abandoned the following summer.

Mystery of Franklin's expedition solved

The failed Belcher expedition was the end of government-sponsored attempts to find out what had happened to Franklin. In the spring of 1854, however, Dr. John Rae (1813–1893) traveled to the Arctic as a physician with the

JOHN FRANKLIN John Franklin was born in 1786 in the village of Spilsby in Lincolnshire, England. He entered England's Royal Navy at the age of fourteen. Franklin fought in the Battle of Copenhagen during the Napoleonic Wars (1803–15). As a young man, Franklin served on ships sent to Australia, South America, the North Sea, and the Arctic. He was later appointed governor of Tasmania in Australia. Franklin commanded three expeditions in search of a Northwest Passage over Canada. On the third voyage, Franklin and his men disappeared. Franklin died on King William Island, north of Hudson Bay, Canada, in 1847.

Hudson's Bay Company. While Rae was exploring the Boothia Peninsula, Inuit inhabitants of the area gave him news about the lost Franklin party. Rae then found possible evidence on King William Island. Encouraged by Rae's findings, Jane Franklin was able to raise enough private funds for one more expedition.

McClintock volunteered to lead the search for free. He left England in July 1857, but did not reach King William Island until 1859. Once there, however, McClintock's sledge teams soon found traces of the Franklin expedition. They even discovered two notes confirming that Franklin had died there on June 11, 1847. McClintock and his party came upon evidence of survivors, including several graves and skeletons, along the western and southern coasts of King William Island. Upon returning to England, McClintock was knighted for having solved the mystery of Franklin's disappearance.

Fate of the final expedition

From notes found by McClintock, historians have constructed a general picture of Franklin's course. He and his men spent the first winter at Beechey Island, then they sailed south to King William Island, where they stayed through the next winter. It was here that Franklin died in June 1847. Unable to free their ship from the ice, the expedition survivors headed down the west coast of the island to try to get across to the Canadian mainland. They hoped to follow the Back River south to Hudson Bay and, with any luck, find trappers and traders along the way who could help them. But all of the remaining men from Franklin's expedition died during this overland march.

Hall's ill-fated search for survivors

Although McClintock had solved the mystery, the Franklin story was not yet over. An American journalist named Charles Francis Hall (1821–1871) had followed news of Franklin's disappearance with great interest. When McClintock found the remains of the expedition, Hall was convinced survivors of the Franklin expedition were still alive in the Arctic. Deciding to test his theory, Hall sold his newspaper in Cincinnati, Ohio, and took a whaling ship to Baffin Island in 1860. He lived with an Inuit couple, Tookolito (called "Hannah") and her husband, Joe Ebierbing, for two years. In 1862 Hall and the Ebierbings went to the United States on a lecture tour to raise money for another expedition. Encountering trouble and hardship, the trio was forced to return to the Arctic, where they roamed for over five years in search of Franklin survivors. Hall's efforts ended in failure. While he managed to find some additional relics from the expedition—including the skeleton of an officer—on King William Island, Hall never discovered any survivors, and he did not find any other places Franklin or his men had landed.

Hall embarked on his final misadventure two years later, when he decided to become the first man to reach the North Pole. In 1871 he and his party set out on a ship named the *Polaris*. Four months into the voyage the group had to take shelter on the northern coast of Greenland. While the ships were in port Hall became ill, suffering for several weeks from hallucinations, nausea, and a high fever. Upon his death the expedition fell apart and all of its members had to be rescued. The U.S. Navy ruled that, in spite of certain mysterious circumstances, Hall's death had been caused by a stoke. Almost a hundred years later, in 1968, Hall's body was dug up for reexamination. Analysis of his hair and nails showed a toxic amount of arsenic (a poisonous element) in the body, indicating he had been poisoned. The most likely suspect in the poisoning is Emil Bessels, a German doctor and the chief scientist on the expedition, who was known to have disliked Hall.

FOR FURTHER REFERENCE

Books

Berton, Pierre. *The Arctic Grail: The Quest for the Northwest Passage and the North Pole, 1818–1909.* New York City: Viking, 1988.

David Livingstone's African Expeditions

JUNE 1849 TO OCTOBER 1873

David Livingstone's

adventures in Africa

were often marked by

frustration and

personal tragedy.

Historians agree that David Livingstone had a great impact on the course of African history. A fervent explorer, Scottish-born Livingstone had many adventures—and experienced serious mishaps—during his years exploring the African continent. He is perhaps most famous for his search for the source of the Nile River, a journey that began in 1865 and ended with the explorer's death in 1873. Livingstone's zeal to investigate new territory often put both himself and his family at risk; he was also impulsive and headstrong in his dealings with fellow expedition members. In the end, however, Livingstone's willingness to endure great suffering for the cause of exploration made him a hero to many of the African adventurers who followed him onto the continent.

A taste for adventure

Livingstone was born in Glasgow, Scotland, on March 19, 1813, the second son of a traveling tea salesman. It was difficult for young Livingstone to get an education, largely because he had to work fourteen hours a day. In his spare time, however, he managed to teach himself Latin, Greek, and mathematics. Livingstone was eventually admitted to the University of Glasgow to study Greek and theology. He later enrolled at the University of London in England and earned a medical degree. During this time he became a member of the London Missionary Society and, in 1840, was ordained a minister. Unable to go to China because of the outbreak of the Opium War between Britain and China in 1839, Livingstone chose Africa instead. He arrived in Cape Town, South Africa, just four days before his twenty-eighth birthday. Livingstone would spend most of his life in Africa, becoming the first European to cross Africa and leading several expeditions to explore the lake system of central Africa.

Discovers Lake Ngami

In 1847 Livingstone and his wife, Mary Moffat Livingstone, moved to Kolobeng, a settlement on the eastern edge of the Kalahari Desert. After a few years, Livingstone became restless. He had often heard about Lake Ngami, a body of water north of the Kalihari Desert, that no European had ever visited. Livingstone decided to go to the lake area, possibly to establish a mission among the Makololo people (a Tswana tribe ruled by a famous chief named Sebituaro). Livingstone was

David Livingstone arrived in Africa a few days before his twenty-eighth birthday. He began his first expedition—a search for the Lake Ngami area—in June 1849.

able to finance his expedition by enlisting the support of a young, wealthy big-game hunter named William Colton Oswell, as well as Oswell's friend Mungo Murray. He set out with the two English sportsmen on his first exploring expedition on June 1, 1849. The men were guided by an African man named Ramotobi who knew the Kalahari Desert well. The expedition consisted of eighty oxen, twenty horses, and thirty to forty porters and drivers. This large troupe often ran out of water, and it was only because Ramotobi knew where to dig that the group survived.

The men saw mirages several times as they traveled. The mirages were sometimes so lifelike that the group ran ahead thinking they had arrived at Lake Ngami. (A mirage is an optical illusion caused by distortions that occur as light passes through layers of air at different temperatures. Many times, a mirage takes the form of a body of water.) At one point,

Ramotobi got lost, but the rest of men were saved when Oswell saw a Bushman woman running away. Oswell was able to catch up with the woman and persuade her to lead the group to a large pool eight miles away. (Bushmen, or "San," are members of a nomadic hunting people located in Southwest Africa.)

On July 4, 1849, the travelers reached a previously undiscovered river, the Zouga (now called the Botietle). Local residents confirmed that the Zouga led to Lake Ngami. Livingstone's party followed the river for two hundred eighty miles, reaching Lake Ngami on August 1, 1849. Unfortunately for Livingstone, the Makololo tribe lived another two hundred miles to the north. The local ruler refused to supply guides to the Europeans for the trip, so Livingstone's party was forced to return to Kolobeng. Livingstone then sent an account of the expedition to the Royal Geographical Society in London, barely mentioning Oswell and Murray. As a result he received his first recognition as an explorer, being awarded one-half of the 1850 royal grant for geographical discovery.

Children put in danger

In 1850 Livingstone tried to reach the Makololo once again. This time he took his pregnant wife and three small children along for the trip. The party's animals were attacked by tsetse flies (parasites that cause sleeping sickness), and two of the children became ill with malaria (an infectious disease characterized by severe chills and fever). Oswell, who happened to be nearby, helped Livingstone's family make it back to Kolobeng. Soon after the family's return, Mary Livingstone gave birth to a baby girl. The newborn also caught malaria and died six weeks later. Livingstone refused to give up, however, even though Mary's mother pleaded with her son-in-law not to take the family any further. He insisted on moving ahead.

This time Livingstone asked Oswell to come with the group; he also proposed taking a different route from the disastrous trip of the previous year. The party set out in April 1851. Oswell killed some fresh game, but there was often nothing to shoot. The expedition's guide, a man named Shobo, turned out to be quite inexpert. He got lost several times, and finally deserted Livingstone altogether. On top of Shobo's desertion, the spare water in one of the wagons was lost in an accident. At one point south of the Chobe River, the party went

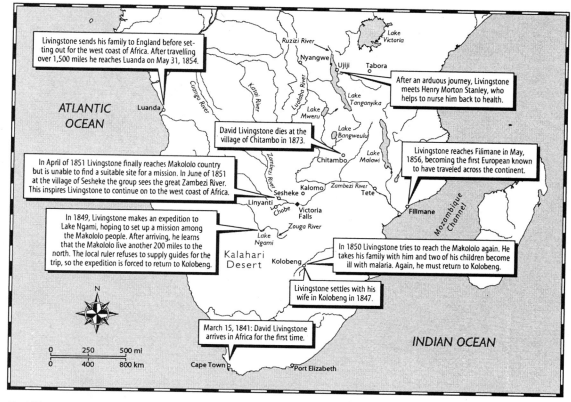

Livingstone sends his family to England before setting out for the west coast of Africa. After travelling over 1,500 miles he reaches Luanda on May 31, 1854.

After an arduous journey, Livingstone meets Henry Morton Stanley, who helps to nurse him back to health.

David Livingstone dies at the village of Chitambo in 1873.

Livingstone reaches Filimane in May, 1856, becoming the first European known to have traveled across the continent.

In April of 1851 Livingstone finally reaches Makololo country but is unable to find a suitable site for a mission. In June of 1851 at the village of Sesheke the group sees the great Zambezi River. This inspires Livingstone to continue on to the west coast of Africa.

In 1849, Livingstone makes an expedition to Lake Ngami, hoping to set up a mission among the Makololo people. After arriving, he learns that the Makololo live another 200 miles to the north. The local ruler refuses to supply guides for the trip, so the expedition is forced to return to Kolobeng.

In 1850 Livingstone tries to reach the Makololo again. He takes his family with him and two of his children become ill with malaria. Again, he must return to Kolobeng.

Livingstone settles with his wife in Kolobeng in 1847.

March 15, 1841: David Livingstone arrives in Africa for the first time.

ATLANTIC OCEAN

INDIAN OCEAN

Kalahari Desert

Mozambique Channel

David Livingstone made several trips into the African interior. During his search for the source of the Nile River, Livingstone became ill and died.

for four days without any water. Livingstone wrote about his children that "the less there was of water, the more thirsty the little rogues became." The travelers were saved when they found the Mababe River on the fifth day. The Mababe, however, was infested with tsetse flies, and forty-three of the oxen died. Four days later Livingstone's group reached the Chobe (or Laiyanti) River, a tributary (or branch) of the Zambezi.

Makes rash decision

Livingstone and Oswell went ahead in a canoe to meet Sebituaro. The chief, who had traveled four hundred miles and was waiting on an island in the middle of the river, wanted guns from the Europeans. He also seemed well disposed to the idea of setting up a mission station in his country. Unfortunately, Sebituaro died from an infection in an old wound less than a month after meeting Livingstone. Traveling northeast through the Makololo country, Livingstone and Oswell looked for a good site for a mission station, but were never able to find one. At the end of June, at the village of Sesheke in what is now Zambia, the men saw a great river—the Zambezi—whose interior course was unknown to Europeans. At that point, Livingstone decided to continue on to the west coast of Africa.

Livingstone and Oswell returned to the Chobe River to get Mary and the three children, then headed back to Kolobeng. Mary gave birth to another child in the middle of the desert. From there the party departed for Cape Town, where they arrived in April 1852. Livingstone packed his family onto a ship and sent them to England, where he entrusted them to the care of the London Missionary Society.

Livingstone almost dies

Livingstone continued north and reached the Makololo country on May 23, 1853. He was greeted by Sebituaro's son and successor, Sekelutu, who accompanied Livingstone on a trip up the Zambezi to look for a site for a mission station. Taking leave of Sekelutu at his headquarters at Linyanti on November 1, 1853, Livingstone traveled into the land of the Barotse people. Livingstone and his supporters went north around Lake Dilolo and through a swampy plain as far as the Kasai River (a tributary of the Congo), which the party reached at the end of February 1854. Livingstone was sick with malaria for most of the time but was well cared for by the men in his caravan. At one point, a local chief demanded that the explorer sell some of the men as slaves in return for food. Livingstone refused, and the expedition was on the verge of starvation.

On March 30, 1854, the explorers stood on a height of land and looked down on the valley of the Cuango River in what is now northeastern Angola. The men were arguing with the people of a nearby village who refused to give them food, when a sergeant in the Portuguese militia appeared and directed them to a nearby military outpost. Traveling by way of Kasange, Livingstone's party reached the city of Luanda, the capital of Angola, on May 31, 1854. In four months the group had covered over fifteen hundred miles of unmapped country. In Luanda Livingstone was housed in the home of the British consul (a government appointee), and his men found jobs on the docks. Livingstone, however, had not found what he was looking for—a site free from fever among receptive people where he could start a new mission.

Rather than taking a ship back to England, Livingstone decided to turn around and on September 20, 1854, headed back inland. The return by a new route proved to be more difficult. It was a year before Livingstone's expedition reached Linyanti on September 11, 1855. As he crossed the Kasai River on his way back, Livingstone recorded that he had suffered his twenty-seventh bout of fever.

Names falls in queen's honor

Livingstone stayed in Linyanti for seven weeks before setting out to travel downstream on the Zambezi on November 3, 1855. Sekelutu accompanied Livingstone for part of the way and furnished him with an even larger escort of porters and guides. Within a couple of weeks after setting out, the expedition came upon the great falls that the Africans called Mosi-AoTunya ("smoke that thunders") and which Livingstone named Victoria Falls in honor of Queen Victoria of England (1819–1901).

After numerous setbacks, Dr. Henry Morton Stanley was able to find David Livingstone in the village of Ujiji in 1871. Stanley's supplies, especially a cache of medicine, saved Livingstone's life.

Continuing eastward, the expedition crossed the Kalomo River into territory inhabited by enemies of the Makololo. From then on they often encountered hostility from the tribes they visited. Livingstone cut across a loop of the Zambezi River, thereby missing seeing the Quebrabasa Falls. His men were saved from starving to death by a party sent out from the Portuguese outpost of Tete in what is now western Mozambique. The expedition reached the port of Filimane on the Indian Ocean on May 20, 1856.

Returns to England

Livingstone was the first European known to have traveled across the continent, and his exploit immediately became famous. A Royal Navy ship was sent out to bring the explorer back to England. When he arrived in December 1856, Livingstone was showered with honors and prizes. The president of the Royal Geographical Society said that he had achieved "the greatest triumph in geographical research ... in our times."

Livingstone eventually resigned from the London Missionary Society, which found his explorations only remotely related to practical mission work. The British government then appointed him consul for the East Coast of Africa and provided him with five thousand pounds and several European assistants. Livingstone was also given a steamer (a small ship operated by steam power), which he named the *Ma Robert*—the Africans' name for Mary Livingstone. In time, all of Livingstone's European assistants died or returned to England. In July 1863 Livingstone was recalled (summoned back) to London; he returned in 1864. The British government was dissatisfied with the results of Livingstone's tenure as consul, and the general public was beginning to ignore him.

A series of disasters

The Royal Geographical Society commissioned Livingstone to return to Africa to continue searching for the source of the Nile. British explorers Richard Burton (1821–1890) and John Hanning Speke (1827–1890) had traveled to East Africa in 1857 and 1858 and come away with differing opinions about the river source. Speke claimed that the Nile almost certainly flowed from Lake Victoria. Not everyone, including Burton, accepted that conclusion. Livingstone believed that one of the sources for Lake Victoria could be found to the south in Lake Tanganyika and that the ultimate source was a river and a lake the local people called "Bangweulu." (Livingstone was wrong. Lake Bangweulu does discharge into Lake Tanganyika, but it ultimately flows into the Congo River system. This was finally explained by Henry Morton Stanley [1841–1904].)

In 1865 Livingstone left England for the last time. He went via Bombay in India, where he engaged James Chuma, a freed slave who had been with him at Lake Malawi. Livingstone then went to Zanzibar, where he hired another freed slave named Susi. In the end, Livingstone was able to find only sixty porters willing to travel inland with him. Everywhere they went, the men saw the results of slave trading. They came upon scores of empty villages full of corpses and skeletons. There was little food to be found, and Livingstone had only eleven half-starved men with him when he reached Lake Malawi on August 8, 1866.

From there the expedition traveled slowly inland to Lake Tanganyika. The journey became a series of disasters: a porter dropped the chronometer (an precise instrument for measuring time) so that Livingstone could not make accurate position measurements. Another porter deserted, taking Livingstone's medicine chest with him. By January 1867 the whole party became ill, and Livingstone came down with rheumatic fever. He wrote in his journal: "I feel as if I had now received sentence of death." He was rescued by a party of Arab slave traders, with whom he traveled to Lake Mweru, which he reached on November 8, 1867.

Livingstone left the traders to search for Lake Bangweulu with only four men. The party reached the lake on July 18, 1868. In his desperate situation, Livingstone's only choice was to go to Ujiji and catch up with the Arabs. Along the way, he came down with pneumonia. When he reached Ujiji on March 4, 1869, Livingstone found that all his supplies had been stolen. For the next year he was sick for most of the time and traveled little.

Stanley finds Livingstone

In March 1871 Livingstone and three faithful attendants—Susi, Chuma, and Gamer—reached the Lualaba River at Nyangwe. The Lualaba flows north (to eventually become the Congo), and Livingstone wanted to believe that it was part of the Nile system. Nyangwe was a major slave trading post, and Livingstone witnessed a massacre when some Arab slave traders fired into a crowded market, killing many innocent people. No longer wishing to depend upon the Arabs and wanting to tell the outside world of the horrors of the slave trade, Livingstone set out with his three faithful companions for a 350-mile walk to Ujiji. When Livingstone reached Ujiji, he had no money and nothing to trade for food. Help, however, was at hand. Susi saw a caravan coming in the distance flying an American flag. Henry Morton Stanley had arrived. The medicine and food that Stanley brought with him were sufficient to restore Livingstone's health.

The Stanley and Livingstone parties set off together to explore the north end of Lake Tanganyika, going farther up the lake than Burton and Speke had been able to do in 1858. The men were able to settle one question about the source of the Nile by finding the Ruzizi River at the north end of the lake, which—contrary to Burton's belief—flowed into, and not out of, the lake. Unfortunately, this led Livingstone to believe even more firmly that the Lualaba River had to be the upper course of the Nile. Livingstone and Stanley traveled together to the major trading center of Tabora in what is now central Tanzania, 300 miles away.

At Tabora Livingstone hired porters in order to make an investigation of the Lualaba while Stanley headed for the coast. He promised to obtain porters and supplies in Zanzibar to send back to Livingstone. Historians have often speculated about why Livingstone did not return to England with Stanley, but there is no definitive answer. In any case, Livingstone waited at Tabora for five months until supplies arrived from the coast.

Livingstone's final journey

On Livingstone's last journey he crossed the Kalongosi River, which flows into Lake Mweru, and headed south toward Lake Bangweurlu. Hopelessly lost and severely ill, Livingstone was unable to walk and confined to a litter. At a village called Chitambo in the district of Ulala the sad little expedition stopped, and Livingstone's final trek through Africa came to an end. After Livingstone's death, his companions—led by Susi and Chuma—cut out his heart and other internal organs, then embalmed (preserved) the body with raw salt. The men buried Livingstone's heart under a tree, then wrapped his body in cloth and bark and slung it on a pole. For eight months the small group carried Livingstone's corpse across East Africa, reaching Tabora on October 20, 1873. There they met an expedition commanded by Verney Lovett Cameron that had been sent out to look for Livingstone. Susi and Chuma turned the body over to Cameron, but traveled with it to the coast and ultimately to England. A large public funeral was held before Livingstone was buried at Westminster Abbey on April 18, 1874.

FOR FURTHER REFERENCE

Books

McLynn, Frank. *Hearts of Darkness: The European Exploration of Africa.* New York City: Carroll & Graf, 1992.

Burke and Wills Seek Telegraph Route

AUGUST 1860 TO JUNE 1861

The Burke-Wills transcontinental expedition proved to be one of the most costly ventures in Australian history.

On August 16, 1860, Robert O'Hara Burke (1820–1861) and William John Wills (1834–1861) embarked on a tragic transcontinental expedition that has become legendary in Australia. Seeking quick fame and fortune, Burke swept Wills up in his grand scheme to find a telegraph route from South Australia to the north coast. The men were able to complete the first stage of their journey, but on the return trip a series of events led to their starvation and death. The Burke-Wills expedition, which accomplished little of value, proved to be the most costly journey in Australian history. The two men became sentimental heroes, however, and their tragedy inspired extensive exploration and development in Australia. Today, the fate of Burke and Wills remains a reminder of an era when adventurers abandoned judgment and caution in the hope of achieving glory.

Expeditions begins in Melbourne

By the late 1850s most of the livable areas of the Australian continent had been explored. Nevertheless, the populated parts of the country had not been linked by a communications system. In an effort to join south and north, the South Australian government offered a reward to anyone who could find a route to build a telegraph line from Adelaide (a city near the southwest coast of South Australia) to the north coast. Accepting the challenge, the rich gold-mining state of Victoria (in southeast Australia) sponsored an expedition that would originate in Melbourne (the capital of Victoria, on the southern coast). As head of the exploring party, the organizers chose Burke, a flamboyant Irish police inspector with a colorful history. His deputy was Englishman Wills, who had studied medicine before becoming a surveyor and meteorologist (a person who observes weather and climate patterns) in Victoria.

Although Burke and Wills had no experience as explorers, they set off with their party amid great fanfare from Melbourne on August 20, 1860. Public contributions and government subsidies had provided ample funds, and the group was given twenty-five camels and three camel drivers for traveling through the deserts of northwest Australia. The men had made seemingly careful preparations for a journey from Melbourne to Menindee, a town on the Darling River in New South Wales, the state directly north of Victoria. Their route would then take them

Robert O'Hara Burke was a rather flamboyant Irish police inspector. Burke was chosen to lead an Australian telegraph route expedition in 1860.

up through the state of Queensland to the Gulf of Carpentaria (an inlet of the Arafura Sea in North Australia) on the north coast of Australia. However, the members of the expedition began to quarrel before they even reached Menindee. One result was that Burke's second in command, George Landfells, resigned and Wills took his place.

Burke becomes impatient

When they finally arrived at Menindee the party was still not fully organized, since the additional men scheduled to join the group had been delayed. Growing impatient with waiting, Burke decided to leave without them. He recruited a local man named William Wright to show him a shortcut to Cooper's Creek, a point on the route four hundred miles to the northwest. Hiring Wright later proved to be one of Burke's major mistakes because he had not taken the time to check out

ROBERT O'HARA BURKE

Robert O'Hara Burke was born into a military family in County Galway, Ireland. Educated in Belgium, he joined a cavalry regiment in the Austrian service at an early age. After serving in the Irish Constabulary (police force), he emigrated to Australia in 1853. Burke then enlisted in the police force in Victoria, Australia, at the height of the gold rush. He was a successful officer, rising to the important post of superintendent of police in the gold-mining district of Castlemaine. People who knew Burke had contradictory opinions of him, ranging from careless daredevil to dedicated soldier. At the time of his appointment as leader of the expedition from Melbourne to the north coast of Australia, Burke was thirty-nine years old.

Wright's reliability. On October 19, 1860, nearly two months after they left Melbourne, Burke, Wills, and three other men— John King, Charles Gray, and William Brahe—moved on toward Cooper's Creek. Guided by Wright, the travelers reached their destination twenty-three days later. Burke then directed Wright to go back to Menindee, pick up the remaining men and supplies, and return to Cooper's Creek. For various reasons, none of which were ever concretely explained, Wright actually ended up delaying his departure from Menindee for three months. This delay would prove deadly for Burke's party in the months to follow.

By December Wright had failed to appear with the additional men and the much-needed supplies, so Burke again grew impatient. He decided that his small crew would continue their journey to the north coast. On December 16 Burke set out on horseback while Wills, Gray, and King rode three of the camels. Burke instructed Brahe to stay behind at Cooper's Creek and wait for their return for three months or until the supplies ran out. The route Burke had chosen skirted the desert—thus making the camels virtually useless—and crossed land already occupied by sheep and cattle stations. The party made good progress at first, but then the rainy season began and the land became a morass of mud. It took the group eight weeks to reach the coast. They were forced to leave the animals behind and forge ahead on foot, finally reaching the mouth of the Flinders River at the Gulf of Carpentaria on February 9, 1861. Unfortunately, they were unable to see the ocean because of the mangrove swamps (tropical evergreen trees or shrubs

Great Misadventures

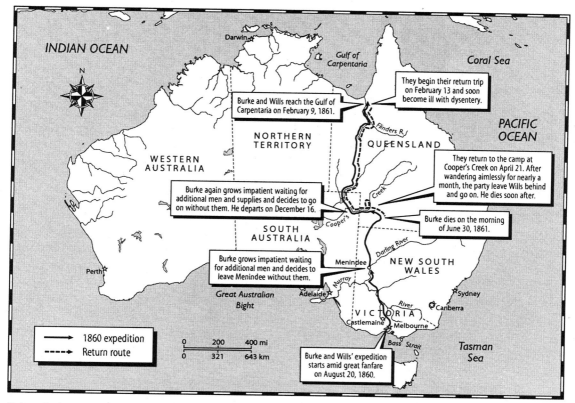

Robert Burke and William Wills set out in search of a trans-Australian telegraph route on August 20, 1860.

having stilt-like roots and stems forming dense thickets along tidal shores).

Concerned about using up valuable supplies during the several days it would take to cut their way through the swamps, the men were forced to turn back. Burke, Wills, and their companions had completed the difficult first stage of the trip—in fact, they had accomplished the goal of the expedition by finding a route to the north coast.

Expedition unravels at Cooper's Creek

After retrieving some of the animals they had left behind, Burke and Wills calculated that they had supplies enough to last five weeks and that the trip back to Cooper's Creek would take eight weeks. (It actually took ten.) The four men left the coast on February 13 in a thunderstorm that would continue for weeks. All the men became ill with dysentery (an infection producing pain, fever, and severe diarrhea) and other diseases. They ate one of the horses, and four of the camels died. On March 25, Gray was discovered stealing rations (food supplies) and Burke gave him a beating. Gray died on April 17. The expedition was quickly unraveling. The three survivors reached the camp at Cooper's Creek on the evening of April 21 and found no one there. Brahe had waited six weeks longer than instructed, but he finally gave up and departed just eight hours earlier. He had left a message carved on a tree directing Burke and his party where to dig to find provisions, as well as a letter telling of his departure. This was a terrible blow to the weary men. On April 22 Burke put a note in the tree at Cooper's Creek for Brahe's party, which he thought was close behind. He stated that he, Wills, and King would follow the creek toward Adelaide but that they were very weak and had only two camels left.

Expedition ends with the deaths of Burke and Wills

Burke, Wills, and King rested for five days before resuming their journey. Along the way friendly Aborigines (native inhabitants of Australia) gave the men food—fish, rats, and nardoo (the seeds of a fern that was pounded to make a kind of flour.) By May 17, the three men had killed their last two camels. Aimlessly wandering in nearly a full circle, by May 28 they were back near the camp at Cooper's Creek where they had started a month before. In the meantime, Brahe had again returned to the camp after encountering Wright, who had at last made his way up from Menindee on May 8. But Brahe left without seeing the letter from Burke or checking to see if Burke, Wills, and King had taken the provisions.

Burke and his crew had meanwhile attached themselves to a group of Aborigines. Soon becoming too weak to gather food, Burke, Wills, and King were abandoned by their wandering benefactors. King tried to supply the other two men with food, but the situation became desperate. Leaving Wills behind with eight days' worth of supplies, King and Burke ventured out to look for the Aborigines. Burke collapsed two days later. King made him a last meal from a crow he had shot and some nardoo. "I hope you will remain with me till I am quite dead," Burke reportedly told King. "It is a comfort to know that someone is by." Burke died on the morning of June 30, 1861.

After burying Burke, King returned to where the men had
left Wills and discovered that he was also dead. At the campsite King found a letter Wills had written to his father, which
began, "These are probably the last lines you will ever get from
me." King buried the corpse in the sand. He was then able to
catch up with the Aborigines, who tolerated his presence and
gave him food. In the meantime, four different rescue crews
had been sent out to find the survivors of the Burke-Wills
expedition. On September 18, 1861, a team led by British-
born explorer Alfred Howitt found King, whose heroic efforts
had kept Burke and Wills alive during their last days. King was
"wasted to a shadow," Howitt reported, but still alive. King
gave Howitt a canvas bag containing watches belonging to
Burke and Wills, as well as Wills's letter to his father and some
notes Burke had scribbled before his death.

Response to the deaths

There was hysterical public reaction in Australia after news
of Burke and Wills's deaths was released. Wills's letter, which
outlined the reasons the expedition had failed, was published
by his father. Many outraged citizens demanded that the
dependents of the dead men be compensated and a grand
funeral be held for Burke and Wills. A royal commission was
immediately assembled to investigate the tragedy. After months

William John Wills served as second in command to Robert Burke during the ill-fated Australian telegraph trek.

of review, however, the commission found that no one person could be blamed.

Burke had made several errors of judgment, perhaps the greatest of them being the appointment of Wright. Wright, who could never explain his delay, was also the subject of speculation. If he had returned to Cooper's Creek with enough supplies, Burke, Wills, and Gray may have survived. Wright was publicly condemned and he retired to obscurity. Brahe had held his post longer than instructed, but he was also criticized because he still had supplies and could have waited for the arrival of Burke, Wills, and King. The commission felt the most fitting punishment for Brahe was the haunting reminder that, if he had waited one more day, the men could have been saved. The commission's report concluded with an expression of sympathy for the suffering and untimely deaths of the men.

Burke and Wills are honored

Officials decided that to appropriately honor the men, their bodies should be returned from Cooper's Creek. Howitt, who had found King, was approached and accepted the task. The bodies were disinterred (removed from their graves) and put in boxes, minus Wills's skull and Burke's hands and feet. The remains were brought back for the funeral held on January 21, 1863. It was a huge affair. Invitations were sent all out over the colony. The funeral car was a replica of the one used for the Duke of Wellington (a popular British military hero) ten years before. The enormous carriage with decorated wheels was drawn by six black horses. An estimated forty thousand people stood and silently watched the procession.

The marker on the grave in the Melbourne cemetery was inscribed with the following words: "In memory of Robert O'Hare Burke and William John Wills, comrades in great achievement, companions in death, and associates in renown. Leader and second in command of the Victorian exploring

Expedition died at Cooper's Creek, June 1861." The people of Melbourne felt the thirty-four-ton monolith (grave marker) was still not enough of a tribute to the men, so a huge monument to Burke and Wills was erected outside the Parliament House, where it still stands today.

Over time, nearly every person involved in the misadventure received a government-approved financial settlement. The Australian government later tallied the total cost of the original expedition, the rescue parties, the funeral, the monument, and the settlements. The final cost was staggering. As the years passed, however, the Burke-Wills expedition—for all its faults—inspired new generations of adventurers. Huge areas of the Australian continent were opened for settlement, telegraph lines were built, and mining became a booming business. The circumstances of the deaths of Burke and Wills were horrible, yet the men's great misadventure had far-reaching effects in Australia for generations to come.

FOR FURTHER REFERENCE

Books

Moorehead, Alan, *Cooper's Creek: The Opening of Australia.* New York City: Atlantic Monthly Press, 1963.

Francis Garnier's Death in Vietnam

DECEMBER 21, 1873

A decorated soldier and explorer, Garnier often let his outspoken and unpredictable nature get him into trouble.

An impulsive tactical move by Francis Garnier on December 21, 1873, helped cause the French to lose control of the Vietnamese city of Hanoi for over a decade. A decorated soldier and brave explorer, Garnier often let his outspoken and unpredictable nature get him into trouble. When he criticized the French surrender to the Germans in the Franco-Prussian War (1870–71), for example, Garnier was demoted (reduced in rank) to a lower post. Even when he was winning, Garnier could not seem to stop himself from going too far. In 1873 Garnier was asked to help free an old acquaintance who was being held hostage by the Vietnamese in Hanoi. Garnier and his men captured the Hanoi fortress with a great show of force. While the Vietnamese were retreating, however, Garnier recklessly led a small party of twelve men in pursuit. As a result, Garnier was killed and French forces lost important tactical and diplomatic ground.

Begins bright career

Garnier (1839–1873) was born in St. Etienne, France. His family was strongly monarchist (they supported the king). Garnier attended the lycée (high school) in Montpellier, then went to the French Naval Academy, where he graduated in 1857. The following year he took part in a French naval cruise that went to Brazil, Uruguay, Cape Horn, Chile, and Tahiti. In the meantime, a war had broken out between China and two Western powers, Great Britain and France. The war was fought over attempts by the Europeans to secure advantageous trade treaties in China. Garnier was assigned to a French warship called the *Suffren*, which left France in 1860 to take part in the hostilities.

During the voyage Garnier distinguished himself by saving a sailor who had fallen overboard. As a result, he was promoted and attached to the personal staff of the admiral of the French fleet. Once in China, Garnier was put in charge of building gunboats to ascend the Pei Ho River and to attack Beijing (the capital of China). He was present when the Imperial Palace in Beijing was captured by the Western allies in October 1860.

After Garnier's success in China, he was sent to Vietnam (then called Annain). France had earlier established the colony of Cochin China, which consisted of the southernmost part of what is now Vietnam,

During his early military career, French officer Francis Garnier distinguished himself with acts of bravery and selflessness.

with its capital at Saigon. The French were constantly engaged in hostilities and negotiations with Vietnamese to increase their influence in the rest of the country. Garnier took part in two small campaigns in 1861 and then returned to France. Bored with garrison (naval base) life in France, he requested another assignment in Cochin China. In 1863 he was appointed "inspector of native affairs" in Cholon. (Cholon is now part of the city of Saigon but was at that time a separate commercial city with a large Chinese population.)

Leads heroic expedition up Mekong River

Once Garnier was in Cochin China, he proposed an expedition up the Mekong River into the interior of China. He wanted to see whether the river could serve as a way of opening up a vast trade area in China for French commercial firms in Saigon. The government approved the idea, but because of

Garnier's junior rank the title of commander was given to Ernest Doudart de Lagrée. Garnier was named second in command and given responsibility for making astronomical, meteorological, and geographical observations on the voyage.

On June 5, 1866, eight Frenchmen, two interpreters, and twelve Vietnamese soldiers and servants left Saigon in two gunboats. Within a month, the group experienced the first of several setbacks. After a brief stop in Cambodia (a country on the western border of Vietnam), they left one of their gunboats behind in Pnompenh (a city in Cambodia). Lagrée's party was able to use the remaining boat for only six days because it was too large for the river. Lagrée and Garnier then decided to travel in canoes made out of tree trunks with a straw roof to protect the men from the sun. As the expedition proceeded up the Mekong into Laos (a country on the southern border of Vietnam), it was halted by the Klion rapids. This was just the first in a series of rapids that interrupted the flow of the Mekong. The men had to travel around each of the rapids through the surrounding forest. They did this so often that they wore their boots out and had to walk barefoot. In April 1867, almost a year after leaving Saigon, the group reached Luang Prabang (the former capital of Laos), where they received a warm welcome.

More hardship

By this time the members of the French expedition were feeling the effects of their travels. Garnier, for example, had almost died of typhus (a severe bacterial disease characterized by high fevers, delirium, headaches, and a dark red rash). The men realized that the Mekong could never serve as a gateway to China, yet they continued on, most of the time traveling overland since they could not navigate the river. By October the group had reached the northeastern limits of Burma (now Myanmar; a country on the western border of China), where they were received by Chinese officials at the small town of Simao. Several great river systems come together in that part of the country, and Garnier heard that the upper course of the Red River was nearby. (The Red River flows into northern Vietnam past the city of Hanoi to empty into the Gulf of Tonkin.) He thought that the Red River might serve as the French route to the interior rather than the Mekong. The Gulf

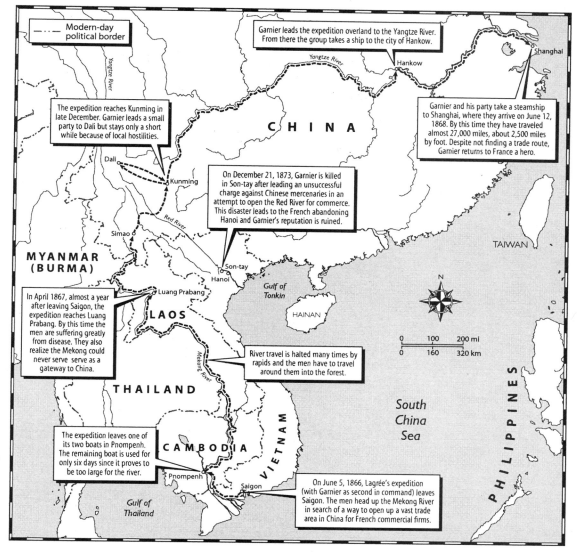

Garnier leads the expedition overland to the Yangtze River. From there the group takes a ship to the city of Hankow.

Garnier and his party take a steamship to Shanghai, where they arrive on June 12, 1868. By this time they have traveled almost 27,000 miles, about 2,500 miles by foot. Despite not finding a trade route, Garnier returns to France a hero.

The expedition reaches Kunming in late December. Garnier leads a small party to Dali but stays only a short while because of local hostilities.

On December 21, 1873, Garnier is killed in Son-tay after leading an unsuccessful charge against Chinese mercenaries in an attempt to open the Red River for commerce. This disaster leads to the French abandoning Hanoi and Garnier's reputation is ruined.

In April 1867, almost a year after leaving Saigon, the expedition reaches Luang Prabang. By this time the men are suffering greatly from disease. They also realize the Mekong could never serve serve as a gateway to China.

River travel is halted many times by rapids and the men have to travel around them into the forest.

The expedition leaves one of its two boats in Pnompenh. The remaining boat is used for only six days since it proves to be too large for the river.

On June 5, 1866, Lagrée's expedition (with Garnier as second in command) leaves Saigon. The men head up the Mekong River in search of a way to open up a vast trade area in China for French commercial firms.

Modern-day political border

In June 1866 Francis Garnier was named second in command of a French expedition up the Mekong River.

of Tonkin, however, was then still in the control of the emperor of Annam.

The French reached Kunming, the capital of the Chinese province of Yunnan, in late December. They found a vast, well-populated land with much natural wealth. However, communication with the rest of China was made difficult by the nearby mountain range. Garnier considered this an even better reason for opening the area to French exploitation. By this time Lagré had become very ill, so Garnier took charge of the expedition. He led a small party to the city of Dali, which was then in the control of Chinese Muslims (followers of the Islamic religion), who were rebelling against rule by Beijing. Garnier and his men stayed only a short while because the city's inhabitants were very hostile. By the time they returned to Kunming in April, Lagré was dead.

Almost 2,500 miles on foot

Garnier led the remainder of the party overland to the headwaters of the Yangtse River, which flows across the entire width of China. The men then traveled by Chinese junk (small sailing ship) to the great city of Hankow in eastern China on the Yangtze. In Hankow Garnier met a French arms merchant named Jean Dupuis. The two men discussed the possibility of using the Red River as a trade route. Leaving Hankow, Garnier and his party took a steamer (steamship) to Shanghai (a seaport city in eastern China). The men arrived on June 12, 1868. By this time they had traveled almost 27,000 miles, about 2,500 miles of that distance on foot. When Garnier returned to France the following October, he was hailed as a hero and awarded gold medals by both the British and French geographical societies. The first International Geographical Congress gave Garnier one of its two special medals of honor—the other went to David Livingstone (see "Exploration and Adventure" entry). Garnier was even received by the French emperor Napoléon III (1808–1873). Garnier was given a special assignment to write the story of his expedition, which was published in 1869. That same year Garnier married a young Englishwoman.

Garnier loses status

Garnier's fall from hero to villain began in 1870, when the Franco-Prussian War broke out. Although he served in the defense of Paris, Garnier strongly criticized the French decision to surrender to the Germans. In retaliation for his outspokenness, Garnier was placed in an obscure post. Taking a leave of absence from the French navy, he traveled with his wife back to China. Garnier financed the trip partly out of his own resources and partly as a correspondent for a leading French newspaper. The Garniers arrived in Shanghai in November 1872. From there, Garnier went alone to Hankow and Beijing, then through central China as far as Kwelchow in the southwest. He returned to Shanghai in July 1873.

A dangerous undertaking

Garnier's undoing came as the result of an urgent telegram from Admiral Dupré, the governor of Cochin China. Dupré informed Garnier that Jean Dupuis, the arms merchant he met in Hankow, had pursued Garnier's advice about following the Red River to the sea. After a series of adventures, Dupuis had collected a force of Chinese mercenaries (hired soldiers) and traveled down the Red River to Hanoi. The Vietnamese government was now holding the men hostage.

Dupré asked Garnier to lead a mission to Hanoi to secure the release of Dupuis and to negotiate the prospect of opening the Red River to commerce. Readily accepting the assignment, Garnier went first to Saigon, where he was joined by a small escort troop of French marines. The group reached Hanoi on November 5. Immediately Garnier began making demands of the Vietnamese commander, who refused to turn over the hostages. In the early morning of November 20, Garnier stormed the Vietnamese fortress with 110 men. At the same time French gunboats bombarded the stronghold with cannon fire. The Vietnamese commander lay mortally wounded as his soldiers surrendered and the French took 2,000 prisoners. In the following two weeks, Garnier sent out a small band of troops who captured neighboring towns and forts.

Garnier's fate

The French met their match, however, when they encountered the large Vietnamese force at Son-tay, upriver from Hanoi. The town was reinforced by a band of Chinese mercenaries and pirates called the Black Flags, who fought off the French troops. On the morning of December 21, 1873, a combined Chinese and Vietnamese army marched under a huge black flag to the walls of the Hanoi citadel. The French cannons were easily able to beat them off. Then Garnier made an extremely reckless move. He personally led a party of only twelve men out of the gates of the fortress to pursue the retreating Black Flags. As he fell into a ditch, he was killed by a volley of spears. Hours later his soldiers retrieved his body. Garnier's head had been cut off and his heart had been torn from his body.

The French abandoned Hanoi after signing a favorable treaty with the Vietnamese. (After 1887, however, Hanoi was the capital of French Indochina.) Blaming Garnier for the loss, the French government refused to award a pension (retirement pay) to his widow, who had been left behind in Shanghai. Over time—as France's hold on Vietnam was more firmly established—Garnier's role in exploring the country and defending French interests was reexamined. His reputation was restored, and he became one of the heroes in the creation of French Indochina.

FOR FURTHER REFERENCE

Books

McAleavy, Henry. *Black Flags in Vietnam: The Story of a Chinese Intervention.* New York City: Macmillan, 1968, pp. 126–46.

George Washington De Long's Search for the North Pole

JULY 1879 TO JUNE 1881

George Washington De Long's misadventure served as a stepping-stone for future polar expeditions.

On July 8, 1879, George Washington De Long set sail on an ultimately disastrous journey to prove it was possible to reach the North Pole by sailing north through the Bering Strait (a body of water that connects the Arctic Ocean and the Bering Sea). Guided by the theory of German scientist August Petermann (1822–1878)—which would later prove to be false—De Long's voyage came to a devastating end when the expedition's ship, the *Jeannette,* was crushed in the ice of the Arctic Ocean. De Long's motivation for his trip was his love affair with the Arctic and his strong desire to reach the pole. The *New York Herald,* the newspaper that sponsored De Long's expedition, did not care about new polar routes or De Long's motivations. *Herald* publishers were more interested in giving their readers a good adventure story. Unexpectedly, *Herald* headlines did eventually announce electrifying news: the tragic deaths of De Long and several of his crewmen.

The polar bug bites De Long

In 1873 George Washington De Long took part in a voyage to search for the ship *Polaris.* The *Polaris,* under the command of explorer Captain Charles Francis Hall (1821–1871), set out to reach the North Pole by sailing up the west coast of Greenland. Hall had died (possibly from poisoning by his own crew) in northern Greenland. His ship then broke up in the ice, although most members of the expedition were saved. Returning from this trip a hero with "the polar virus in his blood," De Long decided to reach the Pole himself using the travel theory of a German scientist named August Petermann. Without any concrete evidence, Petermann hypothesized that at the Pacific entrance to the Arctic Ocean, a warm current of water led to a basin of clear water at the top of the world. It was therefore possible, Petermann argued, to sail on a direct route to the North Pole.

Another factor in De Long's plans was the fierce competition among many newspapers in the United States for circulation. One of the devices newspaper publishers used to attract readers was to sponsor newsworthy stunts (such as setting a travel record). The adventurer doing the stunt would get enough money to cover his or her expenses, while the sponsoring paper would get exclusive rights to the story. The *New York Herald,* for example, had sent Welsh-born American explorer Henry Morton Stanley (1841–1904) to find David Livingstone (1813–1873; see "Exploration and Adventure" entry), an English missionary who was lost in Africa and presumed dead. In an encounter that is still famous today, Stanley found Livingstone alive and well in the heart of Africa. The discovery rocketed the daily circulation of the *Herald* to over one hundred thousand copies. Seeking to capitalize on this success, De Long was able to convince the *Herald's* publisher, James Gordon Bennett, to pay for the costs of an expedition through the Bering Strait to the North Pole.

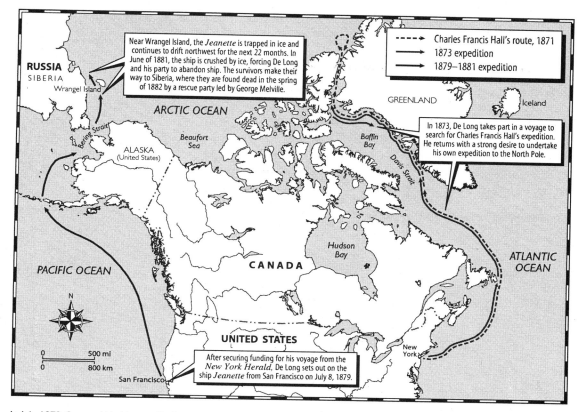

Near Wrangel Island, the *Jeanette* is trapped in ice and continues to drift northwest for the next 22 months. In June of 1881, the ship is crushed by ice, forcing De Long and his party to abandon ship. The survivors make their way to Siberia, where they are found dead in the spring of 1882 by a rescue party led by George Melville.

In 1873, De Long takes part in a voyage to search for Charles Francis Hall's expedition. He returns with a strong desire to undertake his own expedition to the North Pole.

After securing funding for his voyage from the *New York Herald*, De Long sets out on the ship *Jeanette* from San Francisco on July 8, 1879.

Charles Francis Hall's route, 1871
1873 expedition
1879–1881 expedition

In July 1879 George Washington De Long set out on an expedition to prove that it was possible to reach the North Pole by sailing north through the Bering Strait.

Renaming ship invites bad luck

Once De Long had secured the *Herald* as his sponsor, he began preparations for the journey to the pole. Searching for the right ship was a long process, but De Long was finally able to buy the vessel he coveted, the *Pandora*. A collier (a coal-carrying ship) that had been outfitted with sails, the *Pandora* was rechristened the *Jeannette* in honor of Bennett's sister. At the time, naming a polar ship for a woman was unconventional. Most vessels had names such as *Discovery* or *Quest*. Critics suggested that by deviating from the heroic norm and calling the ship *Jeannette*, De Long was inviting bad luck. They warned that the ill-fated British navigator John Franklin (see entry) had changed the names of some of his vessels and the ships were all lost. Sadly, this prophecy would also hold true for the *Jeannette*.

Despite several structural shortcomings which would later become a matter of official scrutiny, the *Jeannette* was equipped with state-of-the-art equipment. Inventor Thomas Edison, who had perfected the electric light bulb, sent a generator to power a masthead lamp, although the generator never actually worked during the voyage. Alexander Graham Bell, the inventor of the telephone, presented De Long with telegraph keys and an underwater cable to establish communications with Siberia and Alaska. With such notable people lending their equipment, the journey was becoming quite an event. In the last weeks before De Long's departure, however, the United States Navy canceled the navy collier that had been assigned to accompany the *Jeannette*. Instead, De Long had to charter the *Fanny Hyde*, an aging schooner (a ship with two masts).

The pressures of planning the journey and coping with the *Fanny Hyde* crisis sent De Long into a depression during his final days at home. "We may be gone for three years," he told Emma, "or we may be gone for an eternity." During one of their last dinners together, Emma wore a black velvet dress. In a chilling foreshadowing, De Long stared at her strangely and said, "I have been thinking what a pretty widow you would make."

Ice crushes the *Jeannette*

Embracing his wife for the last time, De Long left with his crew from San Francisco, California, on July 8, 1879. The *Jeannette* sailed through the Bering Strait and then headed into the Arctic Ocean toward Wrangel Island. (The island is located north of the eastern end of Siberia, which De Long thought to be part of a larger landmass.) Short of Wrangel Island, the ship became trapped in ice and was never able to escape. The ice carried the *Jeannette* northwest for the next twenty-two months. During the Christmas and New Year holidays of the first of two Arctic winters they passed trapped in the ice, the crew tried to improve their spirits by improvising comedies and drinking brandy—anything to break the monotony. Along the way, De Long and his men saw Wrangel Island pass by, an event that proved Petermann's "land bridge to the pole" theory false.

In June 1881, the *Jeannette* was finally crushed by the ice. De Long and his crew of thirty-three men were forced to abandon the ship in three lifeboats. One boat disappeared in a storm, but the other two boats made it to the mainland. Historians have suggested that a much kinder fate might have been for all the men to have died a sailor's death by drowning. Reaching the mainland, De Long and his crew abandoned their boat and trudged through icy mud. In desperation, De Long sent two men out to search for a group of Eskimos. After a horrible journey, the men found a settlement, but their pleas for help were unsuccessful. Frantically, the sailors tried to describe their plight in pantomime (the use of gestures and body movements to describe a thing or idea). Using a child's toy boat and twigs representing men, the men gestured to show that the *Jeannette* was stuck in the ice. Although the Eskimos seemed to understand, they were unwilling to give assistance. This last failure reduced the men to tears. Two weeks later they were found by George Melville (1841–1912), De Long's chief engineer, who had been rescued along with the crew of the other surviving lifeboat. With the Siberian winter having already set in, however, the group had no chance of going out to find De Long and his men alive. Melville and the two men joined the other survivors and returned with the rescue party to England.

De Long and his crew found dead

In spring 1882, *Herald* publisher Bennett sent out a relief party headed by Melville. Unable to run his North Pole story but hoping for a dramatic rescue tale instead, Bennett promised his readers Melville would find De Long "dead or alive." Melville was eventually able to determine the fate of De Long and the others. He found their bodies huddled around the remains of a fire at a campsite on the mainland of Siberia. De Long had his journal flung over his shoulder, probably to avoid the fire that had burned at his feet. His companions had apparently lain directly on the fire for warmth, for their chests were charred from the heat. The men's horrific deaths brought tears to Melville's eyes as he buried them at the site.

De Long is laid to rest

The navy later retrieved the bodies in order to give them a proper burial. De Long still had a flag Emma had stitched, as well as a scrap of the *Polaris*'s flag, which he had planned to deposit at the pole. In his pocket was a battered gold cross, a gift from Emma. Frigid weather followed De Long to the end. It snowed on the day of his funeral, and a naval monument unveiled at Annapolis, Maryland, in 1889 was covered with icicles.

De Long traveled three hundred miles by sledge and boat to the Siberian coast. He proved that the theory of an open-water route to the pole was, as he wrote in his diary, "a delusion and a snare." Although he disproved the theory under horrifying circumstances, De Long was praised for pursuing his quest with little or no concern for his own fate. In fact, De Long's misadventure served as a stepping-stone for future polar expeditions. Three years after the *Jeannette* broke up, some materials from the ship—including a hat and a pair of oilskin breeches that was marked with the name of one of De Long's crewmen—turned up off the southwest coast of Greenland, twenty-nine hundred miles away. This proved that the polar ice was in motion. Norwegian explorer Fridtjof Nansen (1861–1930) then began to speculate whether it might be possible to float on the ice to the North Pole.

FOR FURTHER REFERENCE

Books

Maxtone-Graham, John. *Safe Return Doubtful*. New York City: Scribner's, 1988.

Frederick Albert Cook's "Discovery" of the North Pole

APRIL 21, 1908

Frederick Albert Cook has taken his place in history as the tarnished flip side of Robert Peary's achievement.

American surgeon Frederick Albert Cook began his polar journeys by accompanying American explorer Robert Edward Peary (1856–1920) on a trip to the Arctic. Based on this experience, Cook began thinking about organizing his own polar expedition. To help get the financial backing he needed, Cook fraudulently claimed to have successfully climbed Mount McKinley. The lie worked, bringing Cook the money he needed to support a North Pole trek. Cook left Greenland for the pole in early 1908 and was presumably the first person to reach it, on April 21, 1908. Peary, who reached the pole at a later date, was both outraged by—and very suspicious of—Cook's reported success.

The quarrel between Peary and Cook over the pole made world news. The circumstances surrounding Cook's trip were sketchy at best and he was greeted with much skepticism about the authenticity of his claim. Cook would eventually be labeled a fraud. He had no records of his journey, and had even offered to pay someone for data that would support his claim. When the public discovered Cook's deception, the general reaction was swift and very negative. Even as his fortunes fell, however, Cook continued to take part in shady business deals based on lies and misinformation. In fact, he was eventually jailed for stock fraud, although he was pardoned before his death by President Franklin D. Roosevelt (1882–1945).

135

First American with Arctic and Antarctic experience

Cook's passion for polar exploration began with his surprise acceptance as doctor and ethnologist on Peary's trip to the Far North. After he was unsuccessful in mounting an American expedition to the Antarctic of his own, Cook joined the crew of the Belgian ship *Belgica*. The venture was successful from the outset. The crew conducted important geological (rock and mineral) and zoological (animal) studies during their landings on the Palmer Archipelago (an island group between South America and Antarctica) in January 1898. In February the ship set sail for Alexander Island (an island west of the base of the Antarctic Peninsula).

In early March 1898, the *Belgica* was trapped by ice and drifted for a year to the south of Peter I Island (an island off Antarctica in the Bellingshausen Sea). The *Belgica* was the first ship to spend the winter in the Antarctic, and Cook and the other members of the expedition were the first men to live through such an experience. The sun disappeared for a period of seventy days on May 15. The crew suffered from anemia (red blood cell deficiency) due to their unsuitable rations, and from depression. Daylight returned in July, but it was another six months before the ship could break free to start home in the spring of 1899. During this time, Cook showed a lot of ingenuity. He dug in the snow around the ship to locate seal carcasses for food, sewed warm clothing into blankets, and made a mattress of sealskins to protect the ship's sides from the ice.

Commits first fraudulent act

Even though Cook had endured the Antarctic, he still lacked the necessary influence to finance his own expedition. He joined other explorations whenever he could, but by 1903 he had become discouraged by his inability to set sail on his own expedition. He then trained his sights on Mount McKinley in Alaska, which at 20,320 feet is the tallest mountain in North America. Cook reasoned that if he could conquer McKinley, he could raise the money for his own journey to the pole. Cook led two expeditions to the mountain. The first trek, in 1903, was a reconnaissance (exploratory survey) of the lower slopes. During a 1906 McKinley expedition, Cook claimed to have mastered the difficult southern face of the mountain. Supposedly, Cook and his Alaskan guide, Edward Barille, had been separated from the main party. After a brief absence, Cook

Frederick Albert Cook was the first American explorer with Arctic and Antarctic experience.

reappeared, exclaiming that he and Barille had reached the top on September 16, 1906. Cook even brought back a photograph of himself and Barille with an American flag at the "summit."

The story was immediately met with skepticism. Belmore Brown, a guide who had accompanied Cook on both expeditions to the peak, expressed outright disbelief. His reasons for suspecting Cook was a liar were based on common sense. Cook and Barille were both wearing rubber shoe packs, which were not the proper footwear for going up icy cliffs. In addition, the two men simply were not gone long enough to have completed the trek. After receiving such misleading answers as "You'll have to ask Dr. Cook about that" from Barille, Brown set out to expose Cook as a fraud. Four years later, he found and photographed the actual peak that Cook claimed was the McKinley summit.

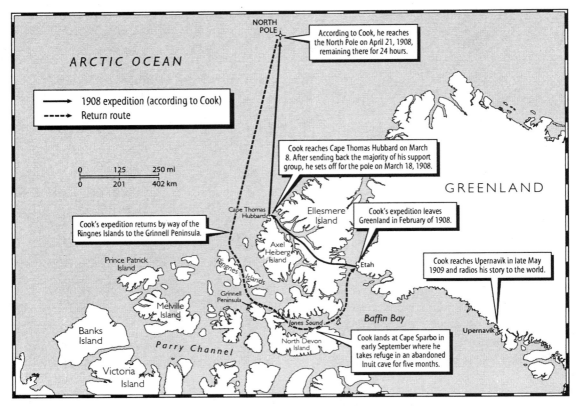

ARCTIC OCEAN

NORTH POLE

According to Cook, he reaches the North Pole on April 21, 1908, remaining there for 24 hours.

1908 expedition (according to Cook)

Return route

Cook reaches Cape Thomas Hubbard on March 8. After sending back the majority of his support group, he sets off for the pole on March 18, 1908.

GREENLAND

0   125   250 mi
0   201   402 km

Cook's expedition leaves Greenland in February of 1908.

Cape Thomas Hubbard

Ellesmere Island

Cook's expedition returns by way of the Ringnes Islands to the Grinnell Peninsula.

Axel Heiberg Island

Etah

Cook reaches Upernavik in late May 1909 and radios his story to the world.

Prince Patrick Island

Ringnes Islands

Grinnell Peninsula

Jones Sound

Baffin Bay

Melville Island

Banks Island

Parry Channel

North Devon Island

Cook lands at Cape Sparbo in early September where he takes refuge in an abandoned Inuit cave for five months.

Upernavik

Victoria Island

In July 1907 Frederick Albert Cook set off from New York City on his North Pole expedition. According to Cook, he and two companions reached the pole on April 21, 1908.

Capitalizes on fraud

In the meantime, however, Cook seized the opportunity provided by his fraudulent mountaineering feat. For a little while, the lie worked. Cook's book about the McKinley climb, called *To the Top of the Continent,* was published by Doubleday. A bit later, Cook was elected president of the Explorers Club. Perhaps the greatest fortune to come from Cook's newfound notoriety was an invitation to lunch with millionaire John R. Bradley. At the luncheon, Bradley invited Cook to accompany him his private yacht on an expedition to hunt polar bears in northern Greenland. After the hunting trip, Bradley suggested, Cook could try for the pole. It was the offer Cook had been waiting for. The two men agreed to keep the "Bradley Polar Expedition" a secret, so that if the expedition was a failure, Bradley and Cook could say it had only been a hunting trip.

Secret expedition exposed

Cook prepared for the Bradley expedition in 1907. Just before Christmas of that year, however, Bradley violated his pledge of secrecy and announced that Cook had 150 dogs and was in charge of a "polar expedition." This news made Peary very angry. The fact that Cook had crept off to the pole without a word to anyone, including his former expedition leader, seemed unforgivable. Peary had nearly reached the pole many times, so he considered himself the real polar explorer. After organizing his own expedition, Peary set out from New York City in July 1907. Cook and Peary were now engaged in a race to be the first man to reach the North Pole.

Cook departed from Greenland in February 1908. His team included Rudolph Francke, an Anoatoak Inuit volunteer, and nine Etah Inuit. (The term "Inuit" refers to the Eskimo peoples of North America, especially Arctic Canada and Greenland.) One hundred and three dogs pulled eleven sledges (sled-like vehicles with long runners) carrying four thousand pounds of supplies. Heading westward, the party reached Cape Thomas Hubbard, the most northerly point of Axel Heiberg Island, on March 8. From there, Cook sent back the majority of his support group, including Franke. With two Inuit named Ahwelahtea and Etukishook, twenty-six dogs, and a collapsible boat, Cook set off for the pole on March 18, 1908. Twelve days later, he claimed to have sighted land to the west, which he named Bradley Land. Later expeditions by other explorers would prove no such land existed.

Did Cook reach the North Pole?

According to Cook, he reached the North Pole on April 21, 1908, after braving the usual hazards of crossing the Arctic ice. Cook stated that he and his two companions stayed at the pole for twenty-four hours before returning by way of the Ringnes Islands to the Grinnell Peninsula on North Devon Island. Along the way they got lost in fog. Using the collapsible boat to travel through Jones Sound, the men reached Cape Sparbo on the north coast of North Devon by early September. There they took refuge in an abandoned Inuit village and a cave the Inuit had carved out of a hillside. Living in the cave for five months, they were able to survive by killing small game with bows and arrows and trapping musk oxen (large, hoofed animals with long, shaggy coats) with lassos. Cook and his men were also pursued by polar bears that practically held them prisoner in their cave. Finally, when the polar night set in on November 3, the bears went into hibernation.

Cook and his associates left North Devon on February 18, 1909, as temperatures dipped to forty degrees below zero. They were able to go by sledge across Baffin Bay and up the coast of Ellesmere Island until they were opposite Greenland. At that point, they had to travel farther north to a place where the ice formed a bridge between Ellesmere and Greenland. The men lived off rotten seal carcasses until they were gone, and then gnawed their sealskin boots and lashings (leather ropes). When they finally reached Anoatoak, Cook's party realized Peary had been through and taken possession of Cook's supply storehouse. This led to hard feelings between Cook and Peary when the two men later returned to the United States.

Peary's journey

Peary had arrived in Greenland on August 18. He then set out from Etah, the home of the Smith Sound Eskimos and the headquarters of the Bradley-Cook expedition. This was where he allegedly raided Cook's supplies. In September, sledging began. Peary believed in living in the open throughout the winter. His men built igloos, but they did not use sleeping bags. Instead, they slept like their commander, in Eskimo sledging clothes on a two-by-four mat of musk ox fur, arms drawn into the sleeves of their deerskin kooletah (heavy coats made for polar weather; also called "anoraks").

Peary's trip had its share of setbacks, including nearly disastrous misconnections and numerous Arctic obstacles. After reducing his crew to six men, however, Peary reached the pole on April 6, 1908—fifteen days before Cook. Peary commented in his diary that the day seemed no different from any other day, nor was the pole any different from any stretch of Arctic wilderness.

Cook tells his story

On Cook's return trip from the pole, he left all his instruments and papers behind in Anoatoak with Harry Whitney, an

THE COOK-PEARY CONTROVERSY CONTINUES

The Cook-Peary dispute over the North Pole has never died out. In recent years there were two major efforts to discredit Peary's claim as the first man to reach the pole. In 1988 British explorer Wally Herbert examined Peary's records and decided that wind-driven ice had pushed him to the west. If Herbert's analysis is correct, Peary—despite his own belief that he had reached the pole—may have never really reached it. In 1989 a Baltimore, Maryland, astronomer made headlines by suggesting that Peary had falsified his evidence on purpose and knew he had not reached the pole. The National Geographic Society then commissioned a study in 1990 that used photographic and other evidence. It demonstrated that, within the limits of his own instruments, Peary was in fact at the North Pole.

American sportsman. Cook then headed south to the Danish settlement of Upemavik so he could tell the world about his trip to the North Pole. Cook reached Upemavik in late May and his story was radioed to the world. By the time Cook arrived in Denmark on September 4, he was being hailed as a hero. Two days later Peary regained contact with the outside world when he reached a fishing village in Labrador. He announced to his patient crew, who had been awaiting his return, that he had indeed reached the pole. Then he relayed the news in messages to his wife, *The New York Times,* the Associated Press, and the Peary Arctic Club. He was too late: Cook had already claimed victory.

Almost immediately, Cook, Peary, and their supporters began slinging accusations at each other. Peary denounced Cook to anyone who would listen. In a cable to the *The New York Times* he stated that "he [Cook] had handed the world a gold brick." Peary's behavior backfired with the public, whose opinion was leaning toward Cook. Peary was openly branding Cook a fraud. In spite of this, Cook seemed to take the high road, publicly congratulating Peary and assuring reporters there was room enough for two at the pole. Many people, however, smelled a rat in Cook's claims.

Cook tried to silence his critics. He stated that, regrettably, he did not have any records. He had left them with Harry Whitney in Anoatoak, he said, fearing his sledge journey would endanger their safety. This notion seemed preposterous, since explorers rarely parted with their records. Ironically, the

Frederick Albert Cook smiles as he leaves Leavenworth prison after serving five years for stock fraud.

"records" had already made the trip back with Whitney, who revealed that instruments—but no diaries— had been left with him. Casting even more doubt on Cook's story was the mint condition of his sledge, which proved that it had never been to the pole. Critics also pointed out Cook's lack of supplies and sledging experience. Still more damaging was the revelation by Ahwelahtea and Etukishook that Cook had merely posed them on top of their igloo with a flag, and the men were never out of sight of Axel Heiberg Island.

Cook's reputation suffers

Cook's reputation crumbled further. In 1910 he had an embarrassing confrontation with Edward Barille in a Montana courtroom on the subject of Cook's McKinley ascent. Although Cook published *My Attainment of the Pole* the following year, the book did nothing to aid his diminished character. Cook then vanished, and his whereabouts were speculated upon as his story collapsed around him. Two New Yorkers, one of them a sea captain, admitted that Cook had approached them with an offer of payment for convincing navigational data that might have been taken at the pole. The University of Copenhagen waited for records Cook had promised, but received only typewritten accounts that gave no computations. In light of this evidence, the Explorers Club dropped Cook from its rolls.

When Peary died in 1920, it was widely acknowledged that he had been the first man to reach the North Pole. During these same years, Cook was viewed largely as a liar and cheat. In 1923 his reputation was further tarnished when he was convicted of stock fraud in Fort Worth, Texas, and sentenced to seven years in jail. Cook spent his remaining years bringing libel suits against his critics. (In a libel suit, a person tries to collect damages—in most cases, money or a public apology—for written or printed statements that damage the person's reputation.) President Franklin D. Roosevelt granted Cook a full pardon for his stock fraud conviction just before Cook's death from a stroke on August 5, 1940.

FOR FURTHER REFERENCE

Books

Maxtone-Graham, John. *Safe Return Doubtful: The Heroic Age of Polar Exploration.* New York City: Scribner's, 1988.

Robert Falcon Scott's Trip to the South Pole

JUNE 1, 1910 TO MARCH 29(?), 1912

"Great God! This is an awful place, and terrible enough for us to have laboured to it without the reward of priority."

—Robert Falcon Scott

Robert Falcon Scott was a famous British naval officer and Arctic explorer who conducted two important expeditions to Antarctica. On the first trip, which lasted from 1901 to 1904, Scott discovered King Edward VII Land (present-day Edward VII Peninsula) and extensively explored the continent. After he wrote *The Voyage of the Discovery* about his travels, Scott was chosen to head a search for the South Pole. In 1910 Scott and his crew set out on a treacherous voyage that was immediately plagued by misadventures, beginning with the selection of an old and unreliable ship. Ultimately, the expedition turned into a race between the British team and a Norwegian party led by renowned explorer Roald Amundsen (1872–1928). Although Scott and his men reached the pole, their achievement was tarnished. The Norwegians had gotten there ahead of Scott's party and placed their flag on the site. On the return trip Scott's team suffered from illness, hunger, and frostbite. Heroes to the last, the men met their deaths in a blizzard just a few miles from the safety of their base camp.

Overcomes hardship on a successful voyage

On January 21, 1902, Scott set out on the venture that earned him fame as an Arctic explorer. He was placed in charge of a specially designed ship called the *Discovery*. The party

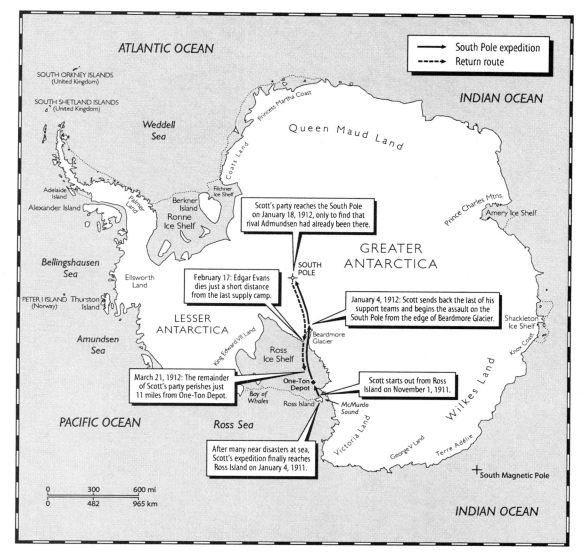

In 1910 Robert Falcon Scott and his crew set out on a voyage to discover the South Pole. Unfortunately for Scott, Norwegian explorer Roald Amundsen had also mounted an expedition for the pole at the same time.

departed from McMurdo Sound on the coast of Victoria Land in Antarctica, traveling east along the north shore of Ross Island to the base of Mount Terror. Continuing to sail eastward, Scott passed the point a previous British explorer named James Ross (1800–1862) had reached. Scott sighted a new land stretching off to the northeast and named it King Edward VII Land for the reigning king of the United Kingdom and

Emperor of India. Extensive ice build up stopped the expedition from going any farther, however, so Scott retraced his path and anchored the ship in a small bay. On February 4, 1902, he went up in a balloon tied to the ship, making the first aerial ascent in Antarctica.

Scott and his party spent the winter of 1902 in huts built at a place named Hut Point on Ross Island. In November he and two companions tried to cross the giant Ross Ice Shelf on sledges (sled-like vehicles with long runners) pulled by nineteen dogs. The men traveled for fifty-nine days until they became so ill with scurvy (a disease caused by lack of vitamin C) that they had to turn back. On their return to camp, they found a waiting British rescue ship. Some of the expedition members were sent back to England in March 1903, but Scott himself stayed until the following year. During that time he explored the ice shelf. In September 1904 he returned to England, where he was welcomed as a great popular hero. His 1905 book about the Antarctic expedition, called *The Voyage of Discovery,* became a bestseller.

Sets out on doomed expedition

Scott was promoted to full captain in 1906. The following year, he heard that Ernest Shackleton (1874–1922), an officer who had been aboard the *Discovery,* was planning to return to Antarctica and try to reach the South Pole. This inspired Scott to attempt the same feat. He asked Shackleton not to use the two camps that Scott's team had established at McMurdo Sound and the Bay of Whales. (The camps would then be available for Scott's future use.)

When Shackleton returned in 1909 without reaching his goal, Scott began organizing an exploring party. On June 1, 1910, he set out for Antarctica with a team of scientists and a naval crew that had been given special leave. The venture seemed doomed from the outset. Scott and his party were sailing on the *Terra Nova,* a whaling vessel that was over twenty-five years old and a drastic contrast to the specially designed *Discovery.* The *Terra Nova* had a history of leaking above and below the waterline. Making matters even worse, nineteen ponies, thirty-three dogs, and three expensive motor sledges (tractor-like vehicles for traveling over snow and ice) were all packed into the cramped quarters of the aging vessel.

Misfortune immediately surrounds venture

When Scott reached Melbourne, Australia, in October, he learned that Roald Amundsen was also leading an expedition to the South Pole. This news did not visibly shake Scott, but it did change the scope of the original expedition. Now, the venture had turned into a race to become the first team to get to the pole. When Scott and his party arrived at Lyrrelton, New Zealand, the *Terra Nova* had to be dry-docked (taken onto land). It had sprung a leak, and everything on board had to be unloaded so repairs could be made. When the expedition was again ready to set sail, the ship was dangerously overloaded. Then a storm hit at hurricane force, loosening bags of coal and hurling them against cases of motor fuel. Faced with the threat of a fire, officers and crew sloshed around the deck retrieving gasoline cans and coal sacks to keep them from breaking open. Below deck, in the engine room, pumps were clogged with coal dust and oil as water rushed through bins where coal was stored. After the storm had died down and the damage was assessed, Scott found he had also lost two of the ponies.

The voyage was further slowed by the heavy load, which made the ship's speed sluggish and caused the engines to burn too much precious fuel. This would be the first of many delays that put Scott's team at a disadvantage in the race for the pole. On January 4, 1911, the men reached Ross Island. Because there was too much ice for the ship to continue onward, the vessel was secured with ice anchors and the unloading began at the point Scott named Cape Evans.

Four hundred miles east, at the Bay of Whales, Amundsen and his men were also unloading. Amundsen's dogs were hitched into teams, but after months at sea, the animals initially refused to pull the sledges. Both the Scott and Amundsen crews were finally able to unload with few mishaps, but then a serious incident occurred in Scott's camp. While being pulled toward shore, a motor sledge fell through the ice and disappeared. This type of incident would be par for the course as the expeditions progressed. The Norwegians appeared to have a charmed existence—what always was good fortune for Amundsen would cause a setback for Scott.

Ponies unsuited for polar climate

A sure sign that Scott's efforts were doomed to failure was his reliance on ponies instead of dogs to pull the sledges that carried supplies. During the autumn and winter, the British set up depots (supply camps to be used on the return trip from the pole) across the Ross Ice Shelf. As they were establishing their southernmost camp, however, the men were caught in a blizzard. The closest camp to the South Pole was to be called One-Ton Depot because of the amount of provisions stored there. Scott had been using ponies to set up the depots, and the inability of these animals to withstand the rigors of the harsh climate became especially apparent when Scot was trying to reach the planned site for One-Ton Depot. Whereas dogs would have been able to travel with speed and vigor over the ice and snow, Scott's ponies bogged down on the ice and suffered in the cold winds.

Although Scott built protective snow walls for his ponies, many were lost or simply could go no farther. Eventually, trugers (snowshoes for horses) were attached to the horses' hooves and the improvement was immediate. There were not enough trugers, however, for all the ponies. Although Scott had ordered several pairs, only one pair had been brought on the trip. If there had been enough trugers, Scott's party could have established One-Ton Depot at its intended position. Instead, because the ponies could travel no more than eleven miles a day, the British had to build the depot thirty miles short of the designated site. This would be an important shortfall for Scott and his team when they returned.

In the race to reach the South Pole, Robert Falcon Scott's British team was pitted against a Norwegian party led by Roald Amundsen. A major factor in the Norwegian victory was Amundsen's use of trained dogs to pull heavy supply sledges. Weighing up to seven hundred pounds, the sledges were loaded with food rations, fuel, tents, sleeping bags, clothing, and other supplies. Amundsen's dog teams easily pulled their heavy loads, running quickly over the ice and snow. Bred specifically for the Arctic climate, the dogs burrowed under the snow to stay safe and warm during blizzards. On the other hand, Scott's ponies had difficulty pulling the cumbersome sledges because their unprotected hooves could not get traction on ice and in deep snow. Moreover, the ponies had no natural protection against the harsh climate, so they suffered at night when temperatures plummeted. Only after several ponies had perished did Scott build snow walls to shelter the remaining animals. In one of the most tragic aspects of Scott's failed expedition, a third of his ponies died. Amundsen's dogs returned home without a single casualty.

Scott makes fatal miscalculation

As the race for the pole gained momentum, it seemed that it took the British three times the amount of time it took the Norwegians to do anything. When Scott finally left for the South Pole on November 1, 1911, Amundsen had a two-week head start. On December 21, 1911, when Amundsen actually reached the Pole, Scott and his men were still traversing the Beardmore Glacier. On January 4, 1912, Scott sent back the last of his support teams. Instead of sticking to his own rule of traveling only in groups of four, Scott added one of the support team members to his team, bringing the group total to five. In addition to Scott, the final party included Edgar Evans, Lawrence Oates (1880–1912), Edward Wilson (1872–1912), and Henry Bowers. This lapse became a crucial factor in the ultimate outcome of the expedition. While there was enough food for one more person, there was not sufficient fuel to cook it.

Death on return trip

Scott and his men began their assault on the South Pole from the edge of Beardmore Glacier, a distance of 178 miles. On January 7 they reached 10,560 feet, the highest point, and started their descent to the pole. The group got there on January 18,

Robert Falcon Scott and four companions died while trying to return from the South Pole in 1912.

only to find the little tent with the Norwegian flag that Amundsen had erected. In a gesture of success and failure combined, Scott's men took a photograph at the pole that shows their strain and disappointment. Scott wrote in his journal, "Great God! This is an awful place, and terrible enough for us to have laboured to it without the reward of priority."

Starting back to their bases on Ross Island, all five of the men in the Scott team were suffering from scurvy, frostbite, and exhaustion. The polar weather that had favored the Norwegians turned bitter for the British. Scott and his four comrades reached Beardmore Glacier on February 7. They took time to collect rock samples, including some with plant impressions that showed that Antarctica had once been forested. On February 17, Evans died a short distance from their last supply camp. It was proposed among the group that any man who could not keep up should kill himself, so opium tablets were distributed. Oates put the plan to the test when his feet were badly frostbitten and one had swollen to twice its normal size. After his companions refused to leave him, he left the tent forever, remarking, "I am just going outside and may be some time."

Scott set up his final camp on March 21, eleven miles from One-Ton Depot. The next day, when a blizzard struck, the remaining men ran out of fuel, so they no food or heat. On March 29, 1912, Scott's last journal entry read, "Every day now we have been ready to start for our depot eleven miles away, but outside the door of the tent, it remains a scene of swirling drift. I do not think we can hope for any better things now." Scott and his two companions were found dead in their sleeping bags by a search party on November 12, 1912.

FOR FURTHER REFERENCE

Books

Maxtone-Graham, John. *Safe Return Doubtful: The Heroic Age of Polar Exploration.* New York City: Scribner's, 1988.

Umberto Nobile and the *Italia* Crash

MAY 1928

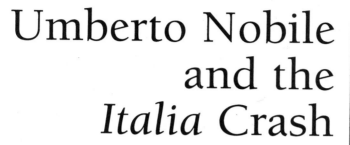

U mberto Nobile was an Italian aeronautical engineer and pioneer in Arctic aviation. Along with Norwegian explorer Roald Amundsen (1872–1928), Nobile flew a successful flight over the North Pole in the dirigible *Norge* from Norway to Alaska. (A dirigible is a self-propelled airship filled with gas to make it lighter than air.) After arguing with Amundsen about who should receive credit for the flight, Nobile vowed to make his own flight over the unexplored Arctic. In his Italian airship *Italia* he embarked on three additional journeys. Each venture was plagued by dreadful weather conditions. The third flight ended tragically when Nobile and his crew were forced to crash-land because their craft could no longer endure some intense storms. Eight lives were lost, but Nobile and the other survivors were rescued.

Compounding the disaster was the disappearance of Amundsen, who had joined the international rescue effort to find Nobile. An Italian commission later found Nobile guilty of the tragedy, forcing him to resign his post. The commission's report would eventually be discredited and Nobile was reinstated to his post. Nobile later published *My Polar Flights*, which chronicled his successes and misadventures in the Arctic.

Umberto Nobile's quarrel with Roald Amundsen led to the *Italia* disaster.

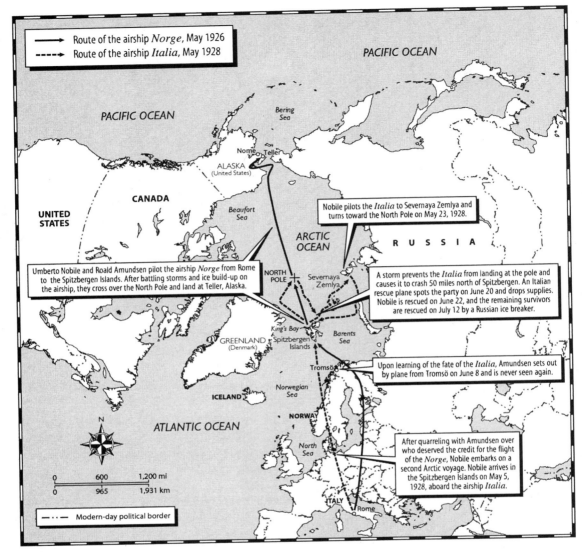

Route of the airship *Norge*, May 1926
----▶ Route of the airship *Italia*, May 1928

PACIFIC OCEAN

PACIFIC OCEAN

Bering Sea

Nome Teller

ALASKA (United States)

CANADA

Beaufort Sea

ARCTIC OCEAN

UNITED STATES

Nobile pilots the *Italia* to Severnaya Zemlya and turns toward the North Pole on May 23, 1928.

R U S S I A

Umberto Nobile and Roald Amundsen pilot the airship *Norge* from Rome to the Spitzbergen Islands. After battling storms and ice build-up on the airship, they cross over the North Pole and land at Teller, Alaska.

NORTH POLE

Severnaya Zemlya

A storm prevents the *Italia* from landing at the pole and causes it to crash 50 miles north of Spitzbergen. An Italian rescue plane spots the party on June 20 and drops supplies. Nobile is rescued on June 22, and the remaining survivors are rescued on July 12 by a Russian ice breaker.

King's Bay

GREENLAND (Denmark)

Spitzbergen Islands

Barents Sea

Tromsö

Upon learning of the fate of the *Italia*, Amundsen sets out by plane from Tromsö on June 8 and is never seen again.

ICELAND

Norwegian Sea

ATLANTIC OCEAN

NORWAY

N

North Sea

After quarreling with Amundsen over who deserved the credit for the flight of the *Norge*, Nobile embarks on a second Arctic voyage. Nobile arrives in the Spitzbergen Islands on May 5, 1928, aboard the airship *Italia*.

| 0 | 600 | 1,200 mi |
| 0 | 965 | 1,931 km |

ITALY
Rome

----- Modern-day political border

Umberto Nobile and his crew made three flights over the Arctic in the airship *Italia*.

Takes first polar flight with Amundsen

Nobile was born near Naples, Italy, on January 21, 1885, the son of a low-level bureaucrat. After studying engineering at the University of Naples, Nobile went to work for the Italian public railways in Rome. He studied aviation in his spare time, and in 1915 was transferred to the Ministry of War. Nobile was eventually put in charge of a project to develop dirigibles. Over time, he produced the prototypes (experimental models) for the most advanced airships and became a world-famous expert in the field.

In July 1925 Nobile was contacted by Amundsen, who wanted him to develop an airship for flight over the North Pole. Financed in part by American explorer Lincoln Ellsworth (1880–1951), Nobile built an airship called *Norge* ("Norway" in the Norwegian language). The *Norge* flew the Norwegian flag, although it was captained by Nobile and most of the crew were Italian. Nobile flew the *Norge* from Rome to Spitsbergen Island off the northern coast of Norway, reaching King's Bay, Spitsbergen on May 7, 1926. Two days after his arrival, American pilot Richard Evelyn Byrd (1888–1957) left Spitsbergen in his airplane to become the first person to fly over the North Pole.

Umberto Nobile was both an airship designer and Arctic explorer.

The goal of Amundsen's expedition was not simply to fly to the pole and back, but to fly across it to the other side of the Arctic Ocean in Alaska. The party set off in the *Norge* from Spitsbergen in the early morning of May 11. On the trip Amundsen and Ellsworth had no formal duties but spent their time observing the polar landscape and making notes. Nobile and his crew navigated and flew the airship. The flight to the pole was relatively easy, although ice was constantly forming on the airship. A large chunk of ice had to be pulled from the air intake duct to keep the ship from crashing. Reaching the North Pole fifteen hours after leaving Spitsbergen, the crew dropped Norwegian, American, and Italian flags over the site.

Difficult return trip

The remainder of the trip from the pole back to Alaska turned out to be the most difficult. The *Norge* was constantly bombarded by ice that formed on the propellers and was then flung loose. One large chunk cut a hole in the hull (the frame-

Roald Amundsen, who once quarreled with Umberto Nobile over credit for a North Pole flight, was one of the first people to volunteer to look for the crashed *Italia*.

work or body) of the airship. When the party reached the Alaskan shore, there was heavy fog and the men could not see the outline of any mountains. Nobile then had to urge the airship to its maximum height in order to fly over unseen obstacles. The *Norge* was knocked around by two heavy storms. At one point it climbed so high that there was danger of the airbag exploding or leaking. Nobile was finally able to land at the small settlement of Teller, not far from Nome. The *Norge* was now in such bad shape that it had to be scrapped. The Amundsen-Nobile party had traveled 3,180 miles on a voyage that took 70 hours and 40 minutes at an average ground speed of 45 miles per hour. During that time Nobile had gotten almost no sleep.

Nobile plans his own flight

Almost as soon as they landed, Nobile and Amundsen quarreled over who deserved the most credit for the flight. Nobile headed back to Rome where he received a hero's welcome from the Italian people and the new Fascist government of Benito Mussolini. (Fascism is a political philosophy marked by extreme nationalism—or duty to the state before the individual—and suppression of opposition.) Largely due to the quarrel with Amundsen, Nobile resolved to carry out an entirely Italian flight over the pole. For the excursion he commissioned the *Italia*, a sister airship to the *Norge*.

The *Italia* crashes

The *Italia* arrived in Spitsbergen on May 5, 1928. Nobile planned to make three flights to unknown areas of the Arctic. After an initial failure, the first flight was made from May 15 to May 18 to the tip of Severnaya Zemlya, an island group north of Siberia. On May 23 Nobile and his crew set out for the North Pole. Although the men reached the pole, bad weather prevented them from achieving their goal of landing there. On

, the return trip, the storm intensified. Twenty hours after leaving the pole the men were forced to crash land on the polar ice. One crew member was killed, and six others were carried off in the crash with the main hull and were never seen again. Nobile and eight companions escaped, but some (including Nobile) were injured.

The group was able to set up a portable camp they had brought with them, including a famous "red tent" that they hoped would be seen from the air. It turned out that the *Italia* had crashed only fifty miles north of Spitsbergen. Nobile sent out radio messages but received no acknowledgment. Then the men heard broadcasts that indicated the search was going on in the wrong area. Three of the men started out over the ice to try reach land.

Nobile party rescued

The Italians saw a rescue plane fly over them on June 17, but they were not sighted by the crew. On June 20 an Italian aircraft spotted the survivors and dropped supplies that day and the next. Finally, on June 22, a Swedish seaplane was able to land at Nobile's camp. The seaplane could only carry out one of the men. After much argument, it was decided that Nobile would go. The pilot planned to return later to pick up the other survivors. On its return to the camp, however, the Swedish plane crashed (although the pilot was saved).

When he reached Spitsbergen, Nobile found that he was being blamed in Italy for the disaster and criticized for being rescued first. In the meantime, the weather had deteriorated, and the spring thaw had begun. It was not until July 12 that a Russian icebreaker was able to reach the remaining *Italia* survivors. Two of the three men who had set out over the ice were rescued. The third man, a Swedish meteorologist named Malmgren, had been abandoned to die along the way.

Found responsible for the disaster

In 1929 an Italian commission of inquiry found Nobile responsible for the disaster. Leaving his native country, Nobile went to work in the Soviet Union designing and making warships. Nobile then spent World War II (1939–45) in the United States helping with the war effort against the Axis powers. (The Axis powers included Germany, Italy, and Japan. These countries were at war with the Allied powers, which included the United States and Great Britain.) When Nobile returned to Italy after the fall of Mussolini's government, a new court of inquiry found that his original condemnation had been politically motivated; as a result, Nobile was cleared of all charges in the *Italia* disaster. He died in Rome in 1978.

FOR FURTHER REFERENCE

Books

Kirwan, L. P. *A History of Polar Exploration.* New York City: Norton, 1959.

The Disappearance of Amelia Earhart

JUNE 1937

No one knows for certain what happened to aviator Amelia Earhart and her copilot Fred Noonan.

The disappearance of pioneering aviator Amelia Earhart remains one of the great mysteries of the twentieth century. A well-known personality during the 1920s and 1930s, Earhart's brief career was filled with record-setting achievements, drama, and excitement. Earhart was drawn to adventure, but the flyer also enjoyed what she called "the beauty of flying." Describing a flight she took from Hawaii, Earhart once wrote, "After midnight the moon set and I was alone with the stars. I have often said that the lure of flying is the lure of beauty, and I need no other flights to convince me that the reason flyers fly, whether they know it or not, is the aesthetic appeal of flying." The disappearance of Earhart's plane over the Pacific Ocean in June 1937 has only enhanced her appeal as a modern-day romantic heroine. Theories about Earhart's fate range from the logical (her plane ran out of fuel and plummeted to the bottom of the ocean) to the bizarre (Earhart spied on the Japanese, then had plastic surgery and assumed a new identit.). No matter what the theory, however, no one knows for certain what happened to Earhart and her copilot Fred J. Noonan.

Buys her own plane

Earhart was born in 1897 in Atchison, Kansas, where she lived with her sister and grandparents until she was twelve

Pilot Amelia Earhart began flying as a young women. She earned money for her first flight lessons by driving a sand and gravel truck.

years old. Her father was a lawyer employed by a railroad company. As a teenager, Earhart lived in various cities, largely because of her father's job with the railroad. In 1918, at the age of twenty, Earhart went to visit her sister in Toronto, Ontario. Toronto was full of servicemen—including pilots—who had been wounded in World War I (1914–18). Like many young women of the time, Earhart volunteered as a nurse's aide at a local military hospital. A bit later, she took a medical course at Columbia University in New York City.

Earhart eventually returned to her parents, who were now living in Los Angeles, California. While at an air show Earhart persuaded her father to spend ten dollars on an airplane ride. The ride confirmed Earhart's love of flying, and she immediately set about arranging lessons for herself. With money she earned driving a sand and gravel truck, Earhart hired Neta Snook— the first woman instructor to graduate from the Curtiss School of Aviation (or flight)— to teach her. After only two-and-one-half hours of instruction, Earhart decided to buy her own plane. A job sorting mail at the local telephone company and a loan from her mother enabled Earhart to buy a small experimental plane for $2,000.

Sets flying records

Shortly after she began flying, Earhart started setting records. Her first record set a new flight altitude ceiling of 14,000 feet. Another pilot soon topped this record, and the determined Earhart immediately tried to set a new one. Flying without instruments, however, she ran into dense fog at 12,000 feet. The flight came close to ending in a crash, but Earhart managed to land safely (though without achieving her goal).

When her parents divorced in 1924, Earhart bought a yellow roadster (a sporty automobile) to drive her mother to the East Coast. In order to pay for the car, Earhart sold her plane to a young man. As she stood watching the plane take off, however, the man immediately crashed and was killed. Back in Boston, Earhart resumed her medical studies for a short while, then became a social worker in a settlement house (or community center). Because of her work and small salary, Earhart had little time or money for flying.

First woman to fly across Atlantic

Earhart's career took a dramatic turn in 1928, when she received an unexpected invitation from a committee headed by the publisher and publicist George Palmer Putnam (1887–1950) in New York City. The committee was in the process of selecting the first woman to travel as a passenger on a plane across the Atlantic Ocean. Earhart was interviewed and chosen. On June 3, 1928, she, a male pilot, and a navigator took off in the *Friendship,* the same plane American explorer Richard Evelyn Byrd (1888–1957) had flown across the North Pole. When the Earhart's flight crew encountered fog, however, they were forced to land the plane in Newfoundland (an island off the east coast of Canada in the Atlantic Ocean) and wait there for two weeks.

The crew's second attempt to fly across the Atlantic was successful. Twenty hours and forty minutes after takeoff, the *Friendship* touched down in a bay in Wales (a peninsula on the west coast of Great Britain), where Earhart and the crew were greeted with great enthusiasm. Although she had been only a passenger, Earhart received international attention because she was the first woman to have flown across the Atlantic.

Becomes superstar

Upon returning to the United States, Earhart suddenly found that she was a spokesperson for female aviators. With Putnam as her manager, she presented lectures throughout the United States and wrote a column on aviation for *Cosmopolitan* magazine. Earhart's name was used to market numerous products, including her own design of traveling clothes, as well as "Amelia Earhart" luggage, which continued to be sold even decades after the pilot's disappearance.

Earhart's reputation as an aviator grew as she continued to set new records. On a trip from New York City to Los Angeles to visit her father, Earhart became the first woman to fly solo both ways across the United States. In 1929 the Lockheed Company presented Earhart with a brand-new Vega, a new type of single-wing plane that was flown by two other famous female pilots, Amy Johnson (1903–1941) and Beryl Markham (1902–1986). Piloting the Vega, Earhart participated in the first Women's Air Derby across the United States. In 1930 she set a new speed record for women.

Earhart later made a tour of the United States in an auto-giro—a forerunner of the helicopter—in which she set an altitude record. Earhart also became the first person to fly from Hawaii to the American mainland, and in 1935 she set a speed record on a solo flight from Los Angeles to Mexico City and another from Mexico City to New York City.

In 1931 Earhart married Putnam. Her fame grew as her husband continued to use his talent to make her one of the best-known personalities in the United States. As a celebrity, Earhart had new and interesting experiences. For example, she took first lady Eleanor Roosevelt (1884–1962) on a flight over Washington, D.C., then escorted her around the White House grounds in a race car.

Solo transatlantic flight

One of Earhart's most celebrated accomplishments was her solo flight across the Atlantic in 1932. Earhart wanted to earn the fame she felt she had not deserved for being a passenger on the Atlantic flight four years earlier. She took off from Harbor Grace, Newfoundland, on a spring evening. For the first few hours the flight went well, but before long Earhart began to have difficulties. The plane ran into a violent electrical storm, the altimeter (a device for measuring altitude) failed, and ice collected on the wings. The plane went into a tailspin and descended 3,000 feet before regaining stability. Just then, the engine caught fire.

Exhausted by these problems, Earhart decided to land in Ireland rather than continue on to Paris, France, as she had planned. She touched down in a pasture outside Londonderry, Northern Ireland, fourteen hours and fifty-six minutes after she had left Newfoundland. Once again Earhart became a celebrity—and this time she felt she had earned it. Earhart's fight won

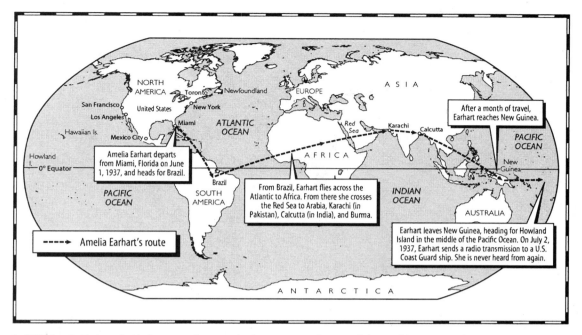

In 1937 Amelia Earhart decided to try to become the first person to fly around the world at or near the equator.

her fame throughout Europe. When she returned to New York City, she was greeted with an extravagant ticker-tape parade. (Ticker tape is the paper ribbon on which a telegraphic instrument prints information such as stock market figures. During ticker-tape parades, spectators toss the ribbons from windows.)

Plans to fly around the world

Five years later Earhart began to make plans for what was to become her final flight. Earhart's new goal was to fly around the world at or near the equator (an imaginary circle around the Earth equal distance from the North Pole and the South Pole), something that had never been attempted. Purdue University purchased a new twin-engine Lockheed Electra specially modified for the flight and university officials presented it to Earhart on her thirty-ninth birthday. In the early morning hours of March 17, 1937, she took off from San Francisco, California, for Hawaii, where her flight was to begin. She set yet another record by reaching Hawaii in just under sixteen hours. As Earhart was leaving Hawaii, however, her heavily laden plane crashed on takeoff. Repairs took five weeks and cost $50,000.

Disappears over Pacific

Because of the delay, Earhart decided to reverse the planned course of her flight. By flying from west to east, she could take advantage of changed weather patterns and air currents. She also replaced her original navigator with the pioneer aviator Fred J. Noonan (1893–1937), who flown the Pan American Clipper from San Francisco, California, to Honolulu, Hawaii, in 1935. Starting their flight in Miami, Florida, Earhart and Noonan took off on June 1, 1937, and headed for Brazil. From there they flew across the Atlantic to Africa and then across the Red Sea to Arabia, Karachi (in Pakistan), Calcutta (in India), and Burma. A month later they reached New Guinea, an island north of Australia. The next part of the trip was the most dangerous because the flyers had to land on Howland Island, a speck of land only two miles long located in the middle of the Pacific Ocean. The size of the island would make it easy to miss.

Earhart and Noonan never reached Howland Island. Earhart sent her final radio transmission July 2 to the U.S. Coast Guard ship *Itsaca,* which was waiting near Howland Island. In her transmission, Earhart stated, "We are on the line of position 157–337. Will repeat this message.... We are running north and south." Putnam immediately mounted a massive sea and air search; he even consulted a pilot who had psychic powers. Putnam's efforts, however, turned up no clues to the whereabouts of Earhart and Noonan. Eighteen months later, Putnam had his wife officially declared dead.

What happened to Earhart and Noonan?

Since the disappearance of Earhart's plane, theorists have offered many opinions about Earhart and Noonan's fates. The most popular theory is that the flyers missed Howland island, ran out of fuel, and crashed into the ocean. In 1992, however, investigators on Nikumaroro, a small atoll (coral island) south of Howland Island, found a shoe and a metal plate that might have been left by Earhart and Noonan. This discovery has fueled the idea that the American government had asked Earhart to spy on Japanese-held islands in the Pacific. According to this premise, the Japanese became aware of Earhart's mission, intercepted her plane, and took her captive. Most experts, however, have remained unconvinced that there is any real proof about Earhart's final fate because her plane has never been found. Nevertheless, Earhart's career and disappearance continue to be the subject of biographical studies, articles, and films.

FOR FURTHER REFERENCE

Books

Kulling, Monica. *Vanished!: The Mysterious Disappearance of Amelia Earhart.* New York City: Random House, 1996.

Periodicals

Morell, Virginia. "Amelia Earhart." *National Geographic.* January, 1998, pp. 112–36.

Christopher McCandless in the Alaskan Wilderness

APRIL 1992 TO AUGUST 1992

Christopher McCandless (c. 1968–1992) entered the Alaskan wild in April 1992 in order to spend the summer alone with nature. During previous travels across the western United States, McCandless had been able to survive on minimal resources; he had also been assisted by people he met along the way. McCandless's success on these treks made him overconfident about his own survival skills. Unwilling to follow the advice of more experienced outdoorsmen, McCandless underestimated the challenges of living in the Alaskan wild. For example, he did not use an updated, detailed area map. If he had done so, McCandless would have seen that help—and a route out of the wild—was not too far away. After surviving for 112 days by foraging off the land, the young adventurer died of starvation. When McCandless's body was discovered and analyzed, the cause of death created a great deal of controversy. Many Alaskans were upset over the young man's apparent recklessness and disrespect for nature. Several other critics pointed out that McCandless had died because he disobeyed the basic Boy Scout motto: "Be Prepared."

A typical American boyhood

McCandless grew up in a middle-class family in Annandale, Maryland. He and his sister, Carine, were given many material and social advantages by their parents, Walt and Billie, who ran a profitable consulting business. McCandless lived in a supportive environment that encouraged him to pursue his own interests. As early as the third grade, a teacher noted that he "marched to a different drummer." In high school McCandless was an honor student and captain of the cross country team. Already showing signs of the independent spirit that would later lead to his death, he encouraged his teammates to see running as a spiritual activity. The boys were "running against all the evil in the world," McCandless once said, "and evil, in return, resisted their doing well."

As a teenager McCandless was especially concerned about hunger in America. He once hid a homeless man in the family camping trailer without his parents' knowledge. But McCandless was not always serious. He had a lively sense of humor and entertained friends with his musical talent. He also undertook many money-making schemes that proved to be highly profitable. Yet, there was also a dark side to the young man's nature. As he grew older he increasingly developed a grudge against his father. Walter McCandless had been married twice—Billie was his second wife—and Christopher never forgave his father for having two children by his previous wife after he had married Billie. In Christopher's mind, his father had committed an unforgivable act of bigamy (marriage to more than one person at a time).

A sense of restlessness

After graduating from Woodson High School in 1986, McCandless bought a Datsun B210 automobile and headed west to California. His parents made him telephone home every three days, and he complied with their wishes until very near the end of the trip. When he returned home two days before he was to report to Emory University in Atlanta, Georgia, his parents were alarmed to see that his appearance had radically changed. McCandless had adopted a scruffy look and insisted on taking his new machete (a large knife) and high-powered rifle to college. Prior to his senior year in college, McCandless took a trip to the Mojave Desert, where he almost died because of dehydration (lack of water and other fluids). He returned home severely underweight. Greatly concerned about the chances their son was taking, Walter and Billie asked

Christopher McCandless took this self-portrait at his wilderness camp.

to be better informed about his future travel plans. As result of this request, McCandless perfected a tactic for handling his parents. He would politely agree with whatever they said, then do as he pleased.

McCandless rejects his parents' values

During his last two years of college, McCandless lived alone in a sparsely furnished apartment without a telephone, making it impossible for his parents to contact him. He withdrew from campus life except for keeping up with his studies. In the spring of 1990 McCandless graduated from Emory with a high grade-point average. At the time, he had a bank account of over $20,000, all of which he gave to Oxfam (the Oxford Famine Relief Fund). Despite their earlier differences, McCandless and his family had a good time at his graduation. Soon after the ceremony, McCandless left on one of his trips, but he promised to return home in a reasonable amount of time. He then drove west.

McCandless wanted to spend enough time in the West to earn money to finance his cherished dream of exploring the Alaskan wild, a goal he called his "Alaskan Odyssey." In a letter to a friend, McCandless spelled out his reasons for adopting an itinerant (wandering) lifestyle. According to the letter, McCandless was looking for adventure, noting that the "joy of life comes from our encounters with new experiences."

Making friends among strangers

McCandless lived for almost two years in the West with little money. Within in a short time, he lost his car. While driving in a forbidden off-road area near Lake Mead in Colorado, he was trapped by a flash flood. Frustrated by his situation, McCandless stripped the car of its license plates. He then burned his money—about $123— and left a note saying that the car had been abandoned and whoever could get it out and running could have it. Park rangers eventually found the car and easily got it started. When no one processed a claim for the vehicle, the park service put it to use making undercover drug buys.

Although McCandless's impatience led to the loss of his car, he was not totally helpless. His ability to make friends quickly led him to an informal support network. Strangers saw McCandless as bright, sociable, and a good storyteller. The middle-class qualities he disliked, such as good social skills, served him well in forming attachments. His new friends were often older and sometimes questioned him about his family. Seldom forthcoming, McCandless ended any conversation that went too far.

Befriends Wayne Westerberg

Prior to leaving for Alaska, McCandless worked in Carthage, South Dakota, for Wayne Westerberg, who owned a grain elevator and operated a combine (a machine that cuts and separates grain) for harvesting winter wheat. Westerberg had picked up McCandless when he was hitchhiking, and the two men became friends. By this time McCandless had renamed himself "Alexander Supertramp," but he introduced himself to Westerberg simply as "Alex." Westerberg could tell that the young man was intelligent and well educated. McCandless proved to be a good worker and no job was too lowly for him—qualities Westerberg admired. McCandless made many other friends in Carthage, especially Westerberg's mother, who admired him because he was true to his beliefs. Since Westerberg was overwhelmed with work, he asked McCandless to delay his departure for Alaska until April 25. Westerberg even offered to buy his young employee an airline ticket to Fairbanks, Alaska. McCandless declined the offer, saying that he wanted to hitchhike.

The misadventure begins

Six days after leaving South Dakota, McCandless arrived at Laird River Hotsprings, 1,523 miles from Fairbanks, near the starting point of the Alaskan Highway. While he enjoyed bathing in the area's thermal pools, McCandless soon realized that he was stranded. Early one morning at the largest pool, he met Gaylord Stuckey, a semi-retiree who was driving a motor home from a recreational vehicle (or RV) manufacturer in Indiana to another RV dealer in Fairbanks. McCandless asked Stuckey for a ride. Although company policy prohibited picking up hitchhikers, Stuckey thought McCandless deserved a lift. He told the young man he would take him halfway to Whitehorse, the capital of the Yukon Territory. Stuckey enjoyed McCandless's company so much, however, that he offered to take him all the way to Fairbanks.

McCandless told the older man about his wilderness plans. Stuckey later recalled that McCandless really seemed to want no part of civilization. The two men arrived in Fairbanks on April 25, stopping at a grocery store to buy a bag of rice. When McCandless announced that he was going to the local university to find a book on edible (safe to eat) plants, Stuckey told him that he would find no vegetation in Alaska at that time of year. Stuckey's concerns mounted as he realized McCandless was determined to begin his adventure in spite of such obstacles. He urged the young man to call his parents, even offering his telephone credit card. But McCandless would not promise anything.

The last man to see McCandless alive

After Stuckey departed, McCandless spent the next three days around Fairbanks making preparations for his trip. He picked up a field guide on edible plants at the university book store, then bought a gun—a semiautomatic, twenty-two caliber Remington with a scope—and four rounds of shells. Camping near the George Parks Highway, McCandless awoke early the morning of April 28, ready to begin the first leg of his journey to the Stampede Trail. As soon as he stepped out onto the road to hitch a ride, a vehicle stopped. The driver, Jim Gallien, agreed to take McCandless to his destination.

Like Stuckey, Gallien's concern grew as he learned about his passenger's plans. Sizing up the situation, Gallien saw a

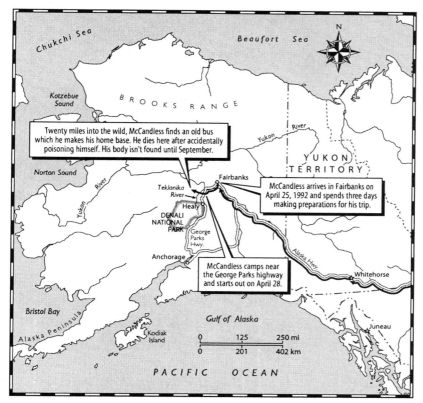

Twenty miles into the wild, McCandless finds an old bus which he makes his home base. He dies here after accidentally poisoning himself. His body isn't found until September.

McCandless arrives in Fairbanks on April 25, 1992 and spends three days making preparations for his trip.

McCandless camps near the George Parks highway and starts out on April 28.

Christopher McCandless entered the Alaskan wild in April 1992 in order to spend the summer alone with nature.

young man ill-prepared for the wild. McCandless did not have the proper gear or food, his state road map did not provide adequate navigational information, and his backpack was far too light (it contained mostly books). Gallien offered to drive McCandless to Anchorage, Alaska, to buy camping equipment, but McCandless said no.

Gallien next tried to scare McCandless out of leaving, but that tactic failed as well. Turning his truck off the highway onto a side road, Gallien drove McCandless as far as he could. He gave the young man a pair of boots, some sandwiches, and corn chips. In return, McCandless offered his watch and all his money—about eighty-five cents. Gallien did not want the watch or money. He took a photograph of McCandless at the trailhead with the camera the young man would use to document his life in the wild. After Gallien left, he thought of stopping in the small community of Healy to inform Alaska State troopers about McCandless's plans, but changed his mind. Gallien was the last person to see McCandless alive.

Makes old bus his home

McCandless entered the bush country with little idea of what lay before him. He proceeded along the Stampede Trail (fifty miles of abandoned road built in 1963), and reached the Teklanika River on his second day. At the river he made a mistake that would have fatal consequences. Although he could easily wade across the river in the spring, McCandless was unaware that when he returned from the wild in July, the water would be a raging torrent fueled by thawing glaciers and melting snow fields.

Twenty miles into the wild, McCandless came upon an old bus equipped with a bunk and some supplies, including matches, near the Sushana River. The bus became McCandless's base of operations for most of his stay in the wilderness. McCandless found that killing small wild game was difficult. On May 9, when he killed a squirrel, he wrote in his journal: "4th day famine." Nevertheless, his hunting skills improved, and for the next several weeks he lived on small game, including duck, goose, porcupine, squirrel, and spruce grouse (a type of plump bird).

McCandless had bragged to Gallien that he was going to walk westward, possibly all the way to the Bering Sea (a distance of five hundred miles). When he left the bus for the sea, McCandless did not know that winter, not summer, was the best time to travel through the wild. The summer terrain presented him with one obstacle after another. McCandless was also unaware of a cruel irony. By Alaskan standards, his trek was in an area that did not qualify as true wilderness. In fact, he was close to the George Parks Highway and Denali Park, which was patrolled by the National Park Service. In addition, he was at all times within a six-mile radius of four cabins. Yet McCandless proceeded as if he were thousands of miles from civilization. After struggling less than fifteen miles, he finally decided to return to the bus.

The dilemma of the moose kill

On June 9, McCandless killed a moose, which weighed 600 pounds or more. Because of its size, the dead animal pre-

WILD POTATO POISONING

Christopher McCandless's death was caused, in large part, by wild potatoes. Although the young man's guidebook indicated that the vegetable was nontoxic (not poisonous), alkaloids (bitter organic substances) became concentrated in the plant's seed coat in late summer. (This happens to prevent animals from eating the seeds.) The alkaloid in the seeds is called swainsomine, a poison that does not immediately kill, but prevents the body from turning food into energy. Ingesting large quantities of swainsomine leads to starvation, regardless of the quantity of food a person eats. As the swainsomine began sapping his body of energy, McCandless became too weak to walk and eventually died.

sented a significant challenge for the inexperienced hunter: how to preserve the meat. The preferred way would have been to cut it into thin strips and air dry it on an elevated rack. McCandless decided to smoke the meat. He had little success, and soon the carcass (dead body) was attracting hundreds of flies and mosquitos, followed by maggots. He then became troubled by the ethical implications of his act, especially the waste of so much potential food. In McCandless's eyes, a true woodsman would not allow a kill to go to waste. The next day McCandless decided to learn to live with such errors in judgment, "however great they may be.".

Trapped and poisoned in wild

On July 3, McCandless decided he was ready to bring his adventure to an end. He reached the Teklanika River only to find it in full flood. He was a weak swimmer, so any attempt to swim across the river was out of the question. If McCandless had walked upstream, however, he would have found that the river broke up into many smaller channels low enough to wade through. Instead, he headed back to the bus.

Near the end of July, McCandless's luck took a turn for the worse when he accidentally poisoned himself by eating wild potatoes. On August 5 McCandless described his weakened condition in his journal by writing that he was "IN WEAKEST CONDITION OF LIFE. DEATH LOOMS AS A SERIOUS THREAT." He continued to live for another thirteen days, killing some small animals, but not enough to regain his strength. McCandless probably died on August 18.

Identified through radio show

Hunters found McCandless's body in September. They called the state troopers, who moved the remains—which weighed only sixty-seven pounds—to the Scientific Crime Detection Laboratory in Anchorage. After an autopsy (a examination of the body), the cause of death was listed as starvation. The police found no identification on the corpse, however, and every physical clue in their possession led to a dead end. It was not until Wayne Westerberg heard a report about the body on Paul Harvey's radio show that he made the connection to McCandless. Westerberg had McCandless's social security number and real name on a tax form, so he called the Alaska State Trooper office. At first, the state police were skeptical because they had received so many crank calls. Nevertheless, Westerberg persisted, and the social security number finally led investigators to the McCandless family.

The meaning of a short life

The reasons for McCandless's sad end can be found in his approach to living in the wild. His previous experiences, even those where strangers bailed him out of desperate situations, gave him a confidence bordering on arrogance about his survival abilities. From the outset, McCandless lacked adequate supplies, food, and clothing for his trip. He had also not taken the time to become acquainted with the geography of the area he was crossing, so he did not know that the spring thaw would trap him on the wrong side of the Teklanika River. Although McCandless had previously lived on little food, he also failed to realize that in the wild, a low calorie intake could soon handicap him. Just as fatally, McCandless dismissed warnings from experienced outdoorsmen about his lack of preparation and the possible dangers he would face. In the end, McCandless seemed to realize that he had made a mistake; by that time, however, it was far too late to save himself.

FOR FURTHER REFERENCE

Books

Krakauer, Jon. *Into the Wild*. New York City: Villard Books, 1996.

Other

Krakauer, Jon. "Death of an Innocent: How Christopher McCandless Lost His Way in the Wilds." *Outside* [magazine]. January, 1993. [*Outside* online available: http://outside/starwave.com: 80/magazine/omindex.html, June 8, 1998]

"Meet the Author: Jon Krakauer." [*Outside* online available: http://outside/starwave.com/disc/guest/krakauer/qa0226alav.html, February 26, 1996.]

Jessica Dubroff's Fatal Flight

APRIL 8, 1996 TO APRIL 11, 1996

"I'll fly 'til I die."

—Jessica Dubroff

Jessica Dubroff was taught to follow her dreams. Her short, unconventional life was greatly influenced by her mother, Lisa Blair Hathaway, and father, Lloyd Dubroff. Hathaway and Dubroff believed that real-life experience was the best teacher. With this in mind, the couple encouraged their children to fully explore subjects and activities that interested them. On Jessica's sixth birthday, for example, her parents gave her an airplane ride. The ride immediately sparked the young girl's interest in flight. True to their beliefs, Hathaway and Dubroff encouraged their daughter to learn how to fly an airplane on her own.

After she had logged only forty hours of flight time, Jessica, her father, and instructor Joe Reid set out on a flight across the United States. The goal was for Jessica to become the youngest recorded pilot to make a transcontinental (across a continent) flight. The media frenzy was astounding as the trio took off on April 8, 1996, from Half Moon Bay, California. Three days later—and three weeks before her eighth birthday—Jessica's plane crashed and everyone on board was killed. In the aftermath of the accident, people began to question the role of the media, Jessica's parents, and her flight instructor in bringing about her death.

JESSICA WHITNEY DUBROFF

Jessica Whitney Dubroff was born in 1989, the daughter of Lisa Blair Hathaway and Lloyd Dubroff, who never married. Jessica had an older brother named Joshua and a younger sister named Jasmine. After Lloyd Dubroff remarried and had another child, his two families lived together near Pescadero, California.

Jessica's short childhood was happy, but unconventional. Her mother was a self-described spiritual healer who believed that real-life experience was the best preparation for adulthood. Hathaway did not let her children play with toys and games. Instead, she taught them how to work with tools and make their own playthings. Jessica and her brother and sister were schooled at home and not permitted to watch television. Reared as strict vegetarians (people who eat only vegetables, fruits, grains, and nuts), the children could not have soft drinks or milkshakes, but drank fruit smoothies (blended fruit juices) and ate health food.

Jessica and her brother were encouraged to work. They did chores in a riding stable in exchange for money and the chance to ride the ponies they tended. Half of Jessica's earnings went to an under-privileged child in India. Jessica and her brother spent most of their time with adults, and many people remember that talking with Jessica and her brother was like having a conversation with another grown-up.

Father plans record-breaking flight

Soon after she received her first airplane ride, Jessica started taking flying lessons from pilot Joe Reid. After nearly four months of instruction, Jessica's enthusiasm for her new hobby had intensified. Then Lloyd Dubroff had an idea: Jessica would set an unofficial world record by becoming the youngest person ever to pilot a plane on a transcontinental flight. Dubroff decided to accompany his daughter, with Reid going along to provide technical assistance. Jessica was thrilled with the prospect of this great adventure. She even wrote a letter to President Bill Clinton, inviting him to ride with her, but the White House declined the invitation.

Dubroff contacted the *Guinness Book of Records,* hoping that Jessica's accomplishment could be entered in the prestigious record book. He learned, however, that the publication had eliminated the "Youngest Pilot" category from aviation achievements in order to discourage accidents. Guinness officials also strongly urged Dubroff not to let Jessica make the attempt (although they reportedly offered to put Jessica's record, if she set it, in the Guinness museum). Nevertheless, Dubroff went

Jessica Dubroff was seven years old when she made her attempt to fly across the United States.

ahead with the plan, raising $15,000 to finance the trip. To commemorate the flight, Dubroff ordered 200 hats decorated with "Jessica Whitney Dubroff, Sea to Shining Sea," which he gave to friends and the media. He then set about promoting his daughter as the greatest aviation heroine since famed flyer Amelia Earhart (see "Exploration and Adventure" entry).

Media circus begins

The media pounced on this unusual and highly profitable human interest story, and television reporters endlessly interviewed Jessica in the days leading up to the flight. Reporters were fascinated by the little girl with a dream who wore a pink flight jacket and a pink baseball cap sporting the words "Women Fly." Although Dubroff freely admitted that the transcontinental trek was his idea, he repeatedly assured the public that Jessica was the motivating spirit behind the project. Reporters followed the preparation of the Cessna, which had to be outfitted to accommodate the tiny pilot. Since Jessica was only four feet, two inches tall, a red booster seat was installed so that she could see out of the cockpit window. A special device also extended the control pedals by three inches so that Jessica could operate the plane. With great fanfare, the major television networks announced that they would cover the flight. The American Broadcasting Company (ABC-TV) even loaned Dubroff a hand-held video camera so he could film his daughter's reactions as she piloted the aircraft.

Jessica's plane crashes

Preparations went according to schedule, and the Cessna took off on April 8. Jessica was in the pilot's seat, Reid was at her side, and Dubroff was sitting behind his daughter. In her wallet Jessica carried an ace of spades playing card for good luck. The flight began without a hitch. On April 10 Jessica completed the first leg of her 8-day, 6,900-mile journey when

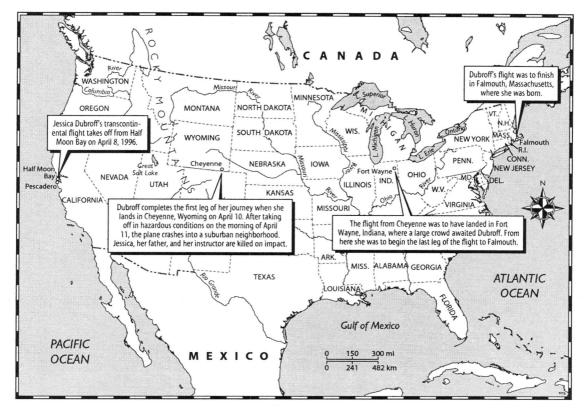

Jessica Dubroff's transcontinental flight takes off from Half Moon Bay on April 8, 1996.

Dubroff completes the first leg of her journey when she lands in Cheyenne, Wyoming on April 10. After taking off in hazardous conditions on the morning of April 11, the plane crashes into a suburban neighborhood. Jessica, her father, and her instructor are killed on impact.

Dubroff's flight was to finish in Falmouth, Massachusetts, where she was born.

The flight from Cheyenne was to have landed in Fort Wayne, Indiana, where a large crowd awaited Dubroff. From here she was to begin the last leg of the flight to Falmouth.

Jessica Dubroff's flight plan took her from Half Moon Bay, California, to Falmouth, Massachusetts.

she landed in Cheyenne, Wyoming. She had had only two hours of sleep. The next day Jessica was scheduled to depart at 8:20 A.M. for Fort Wayne, Indiana, where a large crowd would await her arrival.

An icy rainstorm and thirty-eight-degree temperature made flying conditions hazardous on the morning of April 11. Another complicating factor was the altitude, which is among the highest in the United States. At 6,156 feet above sea level, Cheyenne has thin air, which makes it more difficult for a plane to climb to a safe flying speed. Since heavy thunderstorms were also approaching at more than thirty miles per hour, commercial pilots were delaying airline flights out of Cheyenne.

Reid must have known that flying could be risky in such bad weather, but he decided to takeoff anyway. After a shaky start, the Cessna struggled to reach 400 feet, then wobbled in a circle. It is assumed that Reid had taken over the airplane controls at this point and was attempting to return to the airport. (The Cessna was equipped with dual, or double, controls so that Reid could operate the plane from the copilot's seat, if necessary.) His efforts, however, were unsuccessful. As spectators on the ground watched in horror, the plane nose-dived into a suburban neighborhood. Jessica, her father, and Reid were all killed on impact. The crash site instantly became a shrine to the young pilot, and "Jessica" hats were strewn across the spot where the plane went down. After the initial shock of the crash wore off, however, many people, including members of the media, started asking some disturbing questions about the flight, the flyers, and the role of the Federal Aviation Administration (FAA) in not canceling the trip.

Questions raised

The first question many people asked was: "Why did the crew—especially Reid, an experienced pilot—decide to takeoff in such bad weather?" Critics believe the publicity surrounding Jessica's story contributed to the decision. Everyone expected Jessica to set a record and maintain her schedule. If she delayed takeoff, her record—and publicity surrounding the trip—would be in jeopardy. After the accident, many critics called for stricter media standards in covering the adult-like exploits of children. People were also critical of Lloyd Dubroff for placing his desire for fame and fortune above the safety of his daughter. Yet the most intense criticism was reserved for Joe Reid. Jessica did not make the decision to take off on April 11. Reid, as Jessica's instructor and the official pilot, had a legal responsibility to make the final call. There were many reasons not to leave the ground—the altitude, the weight of the plane, simple routing calculations and checklists that were not completed, and the weather itself. But Reid had clearly ignored all of these warning signs.

Aftermath

An examination of the Cessna Cardinal after the crash found no evidence of any problem with the plane or its engine. In their study of the circumstances surrounding the accident, the FAA emphasized the fact that, under existing guidelines, Jessica was not the pilot and therefore not responsible for what happened to the plane or its passengers. (In the United States, pilots must be sixteen years old in order to obtain a license. Technically, this rule made Jessica a passenger.) In light of the crash—and as a measure to discourage other such flights—the United States Congress passed the Child Pilot Safety Act, which prevents anyone under the age of seventeen from piloting an airplane competitively or attempting to set an aviation record.

FOR FURTHER REFERENCE

Periodicals

Alter, Jonathan. "Jessica's Final Flight." *Newsweek.* April 22, 1996, pp. 24–27.

Howe, Rob. "Final Adventure." *People Weekly.* April 29, 1996, pp. 88–95.

Fatalities on Mount Everest

MAY 10 AND 11, 1996

Hall and Fischer had taken so many people up on Everest that there was a "traffic jam" at the summit.

On May 10 and 11, 1996, seven mountain climbers died when they were trapped in a blizzard on Mount Everest, the world's highest peak. (Some accounts report that eight people died.) The fatalities marked the worst single disaster ever to take place on the mountain. Three climbing teams were descending from the summit (the highest point of the mountain) when the storm hit them by surprise. According to some reports at least ten other groups were waiting out the high winds at various locations on the steep sides of Everest. Most of the climbing groups had a high number of inexperienced members.

The tragedy was especially troubling because it involved teams headed by two of the world's most elite climbers, Rob Hall (c. 1961–1996) of New Zealand and Scott Fischer (c. 1956–1996) of the United States. Hall and Fischer each owned a company that specialized in taking amateur climbers to the Everest summit. The two men were promoting their businesses to potential clients. Hall had recruited Jon Krakauer, a seasoned rock climber and a writer for *Outside* magazine, to write an article on his Everest experience. Fischer had hired New York socialite Sandy Hill Pittman to file on-the-spot Internet (computer network) reports for live broadcast on the National Broadcasting Company (NBC-TV) television network. Pittman's special equipment needs directly contributed to the disaster.

The expeditions were doomed by a simple fact of high-mountain climbing. The challenge is not just getting to the top, but also allowing enough time to return down the mountain safely. Hall and Fischer had taken so many people up on Everest that there was a "traffic jam" at the summit. The teams were then delayed in starting their return trip. The climbers were ultimately undone, however, by an even more basic fact of climbing: the unpredictability of nature. The intensity of the storm was so severe— the wind chill was 100 degrees below zero and visibility was nearly at zero—that the climbers could not follow normal descent procedures. As a result, Hall, Fischer, two guides, two of their clients, and a climber from a third team perished.

Commercialization of Everest

Mount Everest is located on the border of Nepal and Tibet (now controlled by China) in the Himalaya mountains. At 29,028 feet, Everest is the world's tallest peak. On May 29, 1953, a team headed by Edmund Hillary (1919–), a New Zealander, and Tenzing Norgay, a Sherpa mountaineer, were the first men to reach the top. (Sherpas are members of an ethnic group in Nepal who have become indispensable in assisting climbers on Mount Everest. Learning mountaineering skills from their fathers, Sherpas perform most of the essential tasks on a climbing expedition.) Near the summit they encountered an especially difficult obstacle, which is now called the Hillary Step. Everest remained restricted to elite mountain climbers until David Brashears assisted Dick Bass, a wealthy American, in reaching the top in 1985. High-altitude mountain climbing then changed dramatically, giving way to amateurs who had enough money to participate in guided expeditions. Many of these inexperienced climbers had little ability and even less endurance for one of the world's most difficult sporting activities.

Scott Fischer, an experienced high-mountain guide, headed the "Mountain Madness" Everest climbing team. Fischer later died on the mountain.

The challenge of thin air

The major challenge for humans in high-altitude climbing is adjusting their bodies to thin air (the higher the mountain, the thinner the air). The most severe threats are high-altitude pulmonary edema (HAPE; an accumulation of fluid in the lungs) and high-altitude cerebral edema (HACE; an accumulation of fluid in the brain), which can both be deadly and necessitate quick descent. Professional climbers routinely confront these hazards, but the dangers are significantly magnified for inexperienced amateurs. For guided Mount Everest tours, a base camp at 17,000 feet is the starting point where climbers spend three weeks preparing for the ascent. Then climbers stay one night at each of four base camps: base camp one at 19,500 feet; base camp two at 21,600 feet; base camp three at 24,000 feet; and base camp four—known as the "death zone"—at 26,000 feet. From base camp four, the route to the top goes through the South Col (an area known for winds higher than those at the summit), to the Balcony (27,600 feet), to the South Summit, and then to the Hillary Step, which is 200 vertical feet from the mountain summit.

Hall and Fischer teams on Everest

Hall was at the center of the guided climbing phenomenon. As head of Adventure Consultants, Hall escorted thirty-nine climbers to the top of Mount Everest in a five-year period. By 1996 his fee was $65,000 per person and he had no problem finding clients for an expedition that year. Coincidentally, Fischer also planned to lead an amateur team on Everest in 1996. Fischer operated Mountain Madness, a company based in San Francisco, California. Like Hall, Fischer had become a prominent figure in the guided-climbing business. Although Hall and Fischer were leading separate expeditions, they maintained the same schedule for their climbs. By May 10 the two teams had come together in a desperate struggle for survival.

Ascent to the summit

After spending three weeks at base camp one, the Hall and Fischer expeditions proceeded on schedule. On May 9 all but two of the climbers had reached camp four near the western edge of the South Col. (Kruse was suffering from HACE, so he

TWO EVEREST EXPEDITIONS

Rob Hall headed the Adventure Consultants expedition, which consisted of seventeen climbers and six base camp staff members from various countries. For the mountain ascent and descent Hall had employed guides Mike Groom (Australia) and Andy "Harold" Harris (New Zealand). Hall's climbing Sherpas were Ang Dorje Sherpa, Lhakpa Chhiri Sherpa, Kami Sherpa, Tenzing Sherpa, Arita Sherpa, Ngawang Norbu Sherpa, and Chuldum Sherpa (all from Nepal). Hall's clients were Doug Hansen, Dr. Seaborn Beck Weathers, Lou Kasischke, Jon Krakauer (all from the United States), Yasuko Namba (Japan), Dr. Stuart Hutchinson (Canada), Frank Fischbeck (Hong Kong), and John Taske (Australia).

The base camp staff included manager Helen Wilton (New Zealand).

Fischer headed a team of seventeen climbers and four base camp staff members. He had hired guides Anatoli Boukreev (a native of Russia who could climb without oxygen) and Neal Beidleman (from the United States). Fischer's climbing Sherpas were Lopsang Jangbu Sherpa, Ngawang Topche Sherpa, Tashi Tshering Sherpa, Ngawang Dorje Sherpa, Ngawang Sya Kya Sherpa, Ngawang Tendi Sherpa, Tendi Sherpa, and "Big" Pemba Sherpa (all from Nepal). Fischer's clients were Sandy Hill Pittman, Charlotte Fox, Tim Madsen, Klev Schoening, Martin Adams, Dr. Dale Kruse (all from the United States), and Lene Gammelgaard (Denmark).

decided to stay in base camp. He was joined by Schoening, who had a heart problem.) The teams were now preparing for the most grueling and dangerous part of their trek: the ascent to the summit. They would rest at camp four and begin the trip up to the peak the next morning, May 10. Throughout the afternoon of May 9, however, a storm seemed to be brewing and the group was concerned that bad weather would cause delays. Then at 7:30 P.M the wind stopped and the sky cleared. According to Krakauer's account, Hall gave his group an absolute turnaround time (the hour for beginning the return trip) of 2:00 P.M. on May 10. Fischer, on the other hand, set no limits, believing that climbers should proceed at their own pace.

Short-roping Pittman

When the teams started out the following morning, the first problem arose on Fischer's team, when Lopsang Jangbu Sherpa decided to short-rope Pittman. (In short-roping, the climbing harness of one climber is connected with a rope to the harness of another.) Lopsang believed Pittman would never make it to the top without being carried. Moreover, he realized that her ascent—and her promotion of it in the American media—was essential to Fischer. Lopsang had also been toting eighty pounds of Pittman's equipment (a satellite and a computer for relaying reports to NBC-TV). This activity had greatly tired him, and many people were critical of it.

Lopsang's miscalculation would have a significant—perhaps even fatal—impact. He was supposed to be in the lead with Hall's Sherpa, Ang Dorje, to set the ropes. (Setting the ropes involves pounding spikes into the mountain and then attaching ropes that climbers can hang onto as they make their way toward the summit.) Since no one had yet made it to the top in 1996, there were no ropes set that would expedite the ascent. Later, when time was running out just below the South Summit, Krakauer was able to help lay in some necessary ropes with guides Beidleman, Harris, and Boukreev. By 11:00 A.M. Hall's clients Hutchinson, Kasischke, and Taske were lagging behind. When they learned that the summit was three hours away, they decided to go back to base camp. Fischbeck had already returned. Unwittingly, these four climbers had saved themselves from the ensuing tragedy.

Reaching the summit

Fischer's guides Boukreev and Beidleman, Hall's guide Harris, and Krakauer were the first to arrive at the summit. They had reached their goal with some difficulty. It was already past 1:00 P.M., and Krakauer was running out of oxygen. He went ahead to the top of Everest, but he did not stay long because he wanted to conserve oxygen. He did take time to photograph Harris and Boukreev in front of the summit survey marker. On the way down Krakauer met Adams, one of Fischer's clients, who was just coming up. At the top, Adams was the first to notice the formation of thunderheads down below.

As Krakauer and Harris descended to the Hillary Step, they encountered an ice storm. Krakauer de-iced the intake valve of Harris's mask. Then Harris, who had become disoriented, tried to turn off the regulator on Krakauer's oxygen tank to conserve oxygen. In fact, he had turned the valve all the way open. Krakauer was not aware that he had no oxygen at the perilous altitude of 28,900 feet. Since the route was so narrow, Krakauer and Harris had to wait for other climbers to go up the Hillary Step before they could proceed down the South Summit,

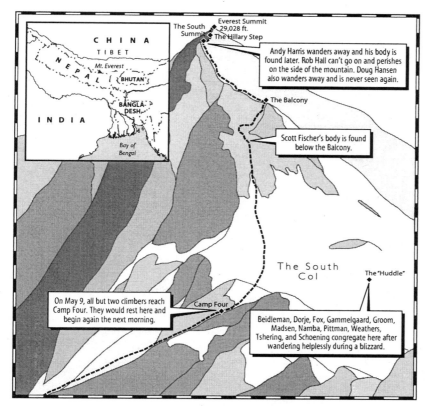

Both Scott Fischer and Rob Hall led Everest teams that included several inexperienced high-altitude climbers.

where additional oxygen bottles were stored. When they met Hall at the Hillary Step, he said that five of his eight clients had already turned back. Weathers had succumbed to blindness, so Hall had told him to wait further down the mountain.

Krakauer and Harris made it down to the South Summit, where they encountered Hall's guide Groom and his client Namba, who were on their way up to the peak. Finally, Krakauer got a fresh supply of oxygen. Proceeding downward, Krakauer and Harris ran into Weathers, who was still waiting for Hall. Learning Groom and Namba were minutes behind, Weathers elected to wait for them.

Victory proclaimed

In the meantime, Boukreev and Beidleman had remained at the summit. By 2:00 P.M., the scheduled turnaround time,

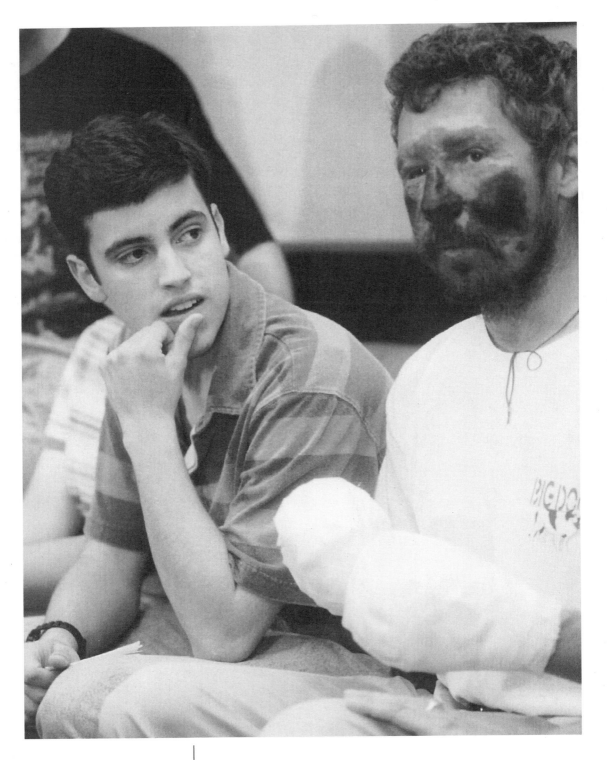

Hall and Fischer had not yet arrived. At 2:10 P.M., the two guides spotted Pittman coming over the final rise. Behind her came other Fischer clients Fox, Madsen, and Gammelgaard. Following them came Hall with his guide Groom and client Namba. Hall radioed base camp manager Helen Wilton to send out faxes worldwide announcing the successful ascent of Mount Everest.

At 3:10 P.M., Beidleman assembled everyone for the trip back down the mountain. Boukreev had already started toward base camp alone. The climbers eventually came upon Weathers and Namba. By now Weathers was blind and could not walk on his own, and Namba, who was out of oxygen, was suffocating because she would not remove her mask. It was 6:45 P.M., and the storm had advanced to hurricane velocity, with little visibility and windchill at 100 degrees below zero.

Death on the mountain

Beidleman and Groom met Fischer's Sherpas Tashi Tshering and Ngawang Dorje and their client Schoening. The group wandered helplessly in the blizzard. They ended up 1,000 horizontal feet from base camp four, where they congregated in what would be called "The Huddle." Now without oxygen, they were more vulnerable to windchill. Around midnight the sky cleared. Although the blizzard continued to blow at ground level, Schoening said he could find his way back to base camp. Pittman, Fox, Weathers, and Namba were too weak to walk, so Madsen decided to stay with them. Schoening led Beidleman, Grooms, and the Sherpas into camp at 12:45 A.M. They told Boukreev where to find the others. He was finally able to rescue everyone but Namba and Weathers, who appeared to be dead. Miraculously, Weathers walked into camp the next day, but later lost his right hand and all the fingers on his left hand due to frostbite. Namba had died.

Fischer dies

Fischer had reached the summit at 3:40 P.M. and found Hall and Lopsang already there. Fischer suffered from a liver condi-

◄Dr. Seaborn Beck Weathers—at one point left for dead on Everest—later lost his right hand and all the fingers on his left hand due to frostbite.

tion, a fact he had kept to himself. Yet it was apparent to guides and clients that he lacked energy on the day of the ascent. Also on the peak was Makalu Gau, leader of the Taiwanese National Expedition team that was on Everest that day. Fischer was suffering stomach pains, so he decided to stop using supplemental oxygen as he started down the mountain. After Lopsang and Gau left, Hall saw Hansen struggling forward. Hansen was exhausted, so Hall helped him to the top. At 4:00 P.M., two hours past Hall's absolute turnaround time, the two climbers were the last to head down from the peak. Hansen was out of oxygen, so Hall radioed Groom, who said extra oxygen was just below at the South Summit. At the South Summit Harris asked Lopsang to take two canisters of oxygen to Hall. Lopsang said he had to find Fischer, so Harris delivered the canisters. By the time Lopsang caught up with Fischer at 6:00 P.M., Fischer was delirious. He urged Lopsang to go on without him and send Boukreev back. The blizzard would make that impossible, and Fischer's body was later found below the Balcony.

Hall fatally trapped

In the meantime, Hall would not leave Hansen alone, even though frequent radio messages from base camp throughout the night urged him to come down. At 4:43 A.M. on May 11, Hall radioed base camp to say he had reached the South Summit and had obtained oxygen but Harris and Hansen were not with him. (Harris wandered away and died; his body was found later. Hansen apparently disappeared because he did not go down to base camp. His body has never been found.) Hall could no longer walk and he was confused. At 5:00 A.M. a call was put through on satellite telephone to Jan Arnold, Hall's wife. Knowing the danger her husband was facing, Arnold urged him to go downhill.

Unable to move, Hall remained in radio communication off and on until 6:20 P.M., when he talked a second and final time to Arnold. Hall later perished on the side of the mountain. Ngawang Topsche Sherpa, a climbing guide for the Fischer team, and Chen Yu-Nan, a member of the Taiwanese team, also died. Since the teams had set out for the summit the previous day, a total of seven climbers had lost their lives.

The aftermath

The shock of the events of May 10 and May 11 dominated worldwide news reports. (For example, a tornado in Bangladesh on May 13 that killed 600 people went relatively unnoticed.) By the end of 1996, at least three other climbers had died on Everest, making it the worst year for fatalities on the mountain. Among the dead was Lopsang Jangbu Sherpa, the lead climbing assistant on Fischer's team. Lopsang died on Everest on September 27, 1996.

Some changes came about as a result of the high death toll. To help gauge storms like the one that hit the Hall and Fischer teams, fax phones are now linked to a British weather forecasting service. On recent expeditions, summit turnaround times have reportedly been enforced. Despite the experiences of the 1996 climbing teams, however, a record number of amateur climbers are still registering for Everest expeditions.

Krakauer eventually wrote his article for *Outside* magazine, which then became the basis of his 1997 book *Into Thin Air.* Stunned and saddened by his Everest experience, Krakauer gave up high-altitude climbing and returned to rock climbing. Boukreev also wrote about the events of 1996 in a book called *The Climb: Tragic Ambitions on Everest.* Despite his bad experience on the world's tallest peak, Boukreev continued to serve as a high-altitude guide until his death in an avalanche on Annapurna (a mountain mass in the Nepal Himalayas) on December 25, 1997.

Almost everyone who survived the 1996 expedition was haunted by what happened to Hall, Fischer, and the other climbers and guides. "It's something you can't fix, something you have to live with," Krakauer told William Plummer of *People* magazine. "But I keep thinking of bringing Doug Hansen's stuff back and handing it to his kids and his girlfriend and his sister.... That's a level of grief I never want to feel again."

FOR FURTHER REFERENCE

Books

Boukreev, Anatoli, and G. Weston DeWalt. *The Climb: Tragic Ambitions on Everest.* New York City: St. Martin's Press, 1997.

Coburn, Broughton. *Everest: Mountain Without Mercy.* Washington, D.C.: National Geographic Society, 1997.

Krakauer, Jon. *Into Thin Air.* New York City: Villard Books, 1997.

Periodicals

Krakauer, Jon. "The Edge of Antarctica: Queen Maud Land." *National Geographic.* February, 1998, pp. 50–57, 61–69.

Krakauer, Jon. "Everest a Year Later." *Outside* [magazine]. May, 1997. [*Outside* online available: http://outside/starwave.com:80/magazine/omindex.html, June 8, 1998]

Parfit, Michael. "Breathless." *New York Times Book Review.* December 7, 1977, p. 24.

Pullman, William. "Everest's Shadow." *People.* June 2, 1997, pp. 53–57.

Picture Credits

The photographs and illustrations appearing in *Great Misadventures: Bad Ideas That Led to Big Disasters* were received from the following sources:

On the cover: *Titanic* sinking (**Painting by Willie Stoewer/UPI/Corbis-Bettmann. Reproduced by permission.**).

In the text: **Corbis-Bettmann. Reproduced by permission:** 4, 19, 35, 202, 218, 241, 284, 378, 389, 410, 447, 455, 468, 544, 586, 603; **Gustave Dore/Corbis-Bettmann. Reproduced by permission:** 10; **Archive Photos. Reproduced by permission:** 16, 27, 66, 97, 150, 153, 411, 412, 418, 436, 622, 652, 725; **Library of Congress. Reproduced by permission:** 42, 48, 105, 109, 231, 372, 406, 448, 464, 494, 565, 570, 578, 581, 588, 592, 628, 651; **The Granger Collection, New York. Reproduced by permission:** 56, 76, 115, 120, 123, 158; **Charles Nahl/Corbis-Bettmann. Reproduced by permission:** 91; **AP/Wide World Photos. Reproduced by permission:** 137, 142, 166, 176, 181, 186, 193, 210, 215, 245, 249, 257, 266, 267, 275, 290, 303, 305, 335, 339, 359, 361, 363, 367, 369, 452, 503, 505, 506, 514, 518, 530, 557, 602, 605, 630, 634, 642, 644, 646, 653, 662, 673, 682, 687, 697, 700, 706, 720, 722; **Norwegian Information Services. Reproduced by permission:** 154; **Lacy Atkins. AP/Wide World Photos. Reproduced by permission:** 176; **Archive Photos/Popperfoto. Reproduced by permission:** 200; **UPI/Corbis-Bettmann. Reproduced by permission:** 205, 226, 326, 544, 547, 616, 654; **Archive Photos/Lambert. Reproduced by permission:** 211; **Lisa Bunin/Greenpeace. Reproduced by permission:** 238; **Robert Visser/Greenpeace. Reproduced by permission:** 296; **Richard Diaz. AP/Wide World Photos. Reproduced by permission:** 303; **Peter Maksymec/AP/Wide World Photos.**

Index

Italic type indicates volume numbers; boldface type indicates entries and their page numbers; (ill.) indicates illustrations.

C

C-16 Organized Crime Squad *4:* 684–85, 687, 688

CAA (Civil Aeronautics Administration) *2:* 259

CAB (Civil Aeronautics Board) *2:* 262–263

Cabeza de Vaca, Alvar Nuñez *1:* 34

Caesar and Cleopatra 4: 564

Caesarion *4:* 563

California Gold Rush *4:* 724

Californian 2: 206

Calley, William L. *3:* 541

Callisthenes *3:* 380

Calpurnia *4:* 563

Cameron, James *4:* 667

Cameron, Verney Lovett *1:* 113

Cantrill, Hadley *4:* 625

Carney, William H. *3:* 451

Carpathia 2: 206

Carrel, Alexis *2:* 214

Carson, Rachel *2:* 230, 232–34

Carter, Jimmy *2:* 238, 240, 242, 300; *3:* 546, 554

Cartolini, Nestor Cerpa *4:* 717–19, 722, 723

Casement, Roger *3:* 488, 491, 492, 492 (ill.), 494

Cass, Lewis *3:* 420–22

Castellano, Paul *4:* 689

Castro, Fidel *3:* 529, 530 (ill.), 531, 533

Catesby, Robert *4:* 580–82

Cayacauga 3: 417–19

Ceannt, Eamonn *3:* 489

Cecil, Edward *3:* 393, 395, 398

Center for the Biology of Natural Systems *2:* 280

Central Powers *3:* 470

CERN (European Laboratory for Particle Research) *2:* 314

Challenger explosion *2:* **320–30,** 321 (ill.), 326 (ill.)

Chambers, Whittaker *4:* 628

Chapin, Dwight *4:* 656

Charles I *4:* 580

Charles of Spain *1:* 29, 31

Charles XII *3:* 400–02

Chase, Hal *4:* 609

Chaves, Steve *4:* 672

Chemical dispersants *2:* 340

Chemie Grünenthal *2:* 254–55

Chernobyl accident *2:* **331–37,** 335 (ill.)

Chevrolet Corvair *2:* **265–72,** 266 (ill.)

Chiang Kai-shek *4:* 629

Chicago White Sox *4:* 607, 610, 614

Chicksika *3:* 410

Child Pilot Safety Act *1:* 179

Children's Crusade *1:* **7–13,** 10 (ill.)

Christmas Island *1:* 73

Chrysler Valiant *2:* 267

Chuma, James *1:* 110, 113

Churchill, Winston *3:* 500

Chuvakhin, Sergei *4:* 677, 678, 681

CIA (Central Intelligence Agency) *3:* 529, 532–34, 553, 558; *4:* 675, 680–83

Cicotte, Eddie *4:* 608, 610

Cimino, Michael *4:* 661, 662

Cincinnati Reds *4:* 607–09, 613, 614

Cirelli, Michael *4:* 686

Citizen Army *3:* 489

Citizen Kane 4: 624

Clark, William *1:* 89

Clark, Barney *2:* 214, 218 (ill.)

Clarke, Thomas *3:* 489–91

Clean Sox *4:* 607, 614

Cleopatra's fall *4:* **561–66,** 562 (ill.)

The Climb: Tragic Ambitions on Everest 1: 189

Clinton, Bill *1:* 175; *2:* 312, 349; *4:* 670

Clitus *3:* 380

CNN (Cable News Network) *3:* 558

Cobb, Ty *4:* 609, 613

Coiro, Michael *4:* 687

Colbern, Lawrence *3:* 541

Cold War (definition) *4:* 678

Collins, Michael *3:* 493

Collinson, Richard *1:* 98

Colorado River *1:* 87, 88

Colson, Charles *4:* 656

Columbia River Territory *1:* 87–88

Columbia 2: 322

Columbus, Bartholomeo *1:* 19, 21

Columbus, Christopher *1:* **14–23,** 16 (ill.)

Columbus, Diego *1:* 22

Columbus, Fernando *1:* 19, 22

Comiskey, Charles *4:* 607, 610–12

Commoner, Barry *2:* 280

Communism *3:* 521–23, 527, 539, 543

Communist Party *4:* 627–29, 635, 638

Confederacy *3:* 454, 462, 463–64

Confederate States of America *3:* 446

Connally, John *4:* 656

Connolly, James *3:* 489, 491, 493

Conquistadors (definition) *1:* 24

Continental Army *3:* 406

Contras *3:* 551

Cook Strait *1:* 68

Cook, Frederick Albert *1:* **135–43,** 137 (ill.), 142 (ill.)

Cook, James *1:* **65–74,** 66 (ill.)

Cooley, Denton *2:* 215

Cooper's Creek *1:* 115, 117, 118, 120

Copper mining in Butte, Montana *2:* **191–97**

Holy City 1: 8

Holy Land 1: 8–9, 11, 12; 3: 386, 387, 392

Hooker Chemical Corporation 2: 237, 240, 241

Hopper, Dennis 4: 665

Hospital for Sick Children 4: 615

Hostage crisis in Peru 4: 717–23, 720 (ill.), 722 (ill.)

Houghton, Daniel 1: 76–77

House Un-American Activities Committee 4: 628, 629

Howard Hughes Medical Institute 2: 251

Howard, Edward Lee 4: 679

Howe, William 3: 406

Howitt, Alfred 1: 119, 120

Hudson's Bay Company 1: 83, 88–89

Hugh IX 3: 391

Hugh VIII 3: 391

Hugh X 3: 391

Hughes Aircraft Company 2: 246, 251

Hughes Tool Company 2: 244

Hughes, Howard 2: 244–52, 245 (ill.)

Hull, William 3: 415, 417, 418 (ill.)

Humboldt River 1: 87

Hundred Days 3: 427, 432

Hunter Commission 3: 496, 500

Hurricane Grace 4: 691

Hussein, Saddam 3: 553, 560

Hutchinson, Stuart 1: 183, 184

I

Idaho National Engineering Laboratory 2: 301

ILGW (International Ladies Garment Workers) 4: 606

Incans 1: 24, 28

Indian Supreme Court 2: 317

Industrial Revolution 4: 585–87

Infantry charge 3: 430

Innocent III 1: 9

Institute of Nuclear Power Operations (INPO) 2: 301

Inter-American Commission on Human Rights 4: 719

International Ice Patrol 2: 198, 207

Into Thin Air 1: 189, 190

Intrepid 1: 101

Invasion from Mars 4: 625

Investigator 1: 98–100

Iran-Contra affair 3: 551

Iran hostages 3: 546– 547, 547 (ill.)

Iran-Iraq war 3: 555

Irish Republican Army 3: 493

Irish Republican Brotherhood 3: 489

Irish Volunteers 3: 489, 3: 490

Iron Hugo 1: 11

Iroquois 1: 59

Irving, Clifford 2: 251

Isaaco 1: 79

Isabella, Queen 1: 16, 21, 22

Ishii, Tomoko 4: 712

Ismay, J. Bruce 2: 199, 202

The *Italia* crash 1: 151–56

Itsaca 1: 162

Iwo Jima 2: 287

IWW (*International Workers of the World*) 2: 191, 194

J

Morgan, J. P. 4: 727

Jackson, Andrew 3: 424

Jackson, Joe ("Shoeless Joe") 4: 608–10, 614

Jackson, Thomas "Stonewall" 3: 456, 457

Jager, Peter de 2: 346

James I 1: 44; 4: 580–81, 581 (ill.)

Jarvik, Robert 2: 215 (ill.), 216, 217

Jarvik-7 2: 214, 218, 219

Jarvik-3 2: 217

Jarvis, Gregory 2: 324

Jaworski, Leon 4: 655–57

Jeannette 1: 129, 131–34

Jefferson, Thomas 3: 418

Jenkinson, Robert Banks 4: 589

Jersey Central Power and Light Company 2: 296

Jesus of Nazareth 1: 7, 8

Jett, Joseph 4: 709

John Brown's raid 3: 595–99

Johnson, Lyndon B. 2: 270; 3: 538, 542; 4: 659

Jolliet, Louis 1: 59, 62

Joséphine 3: 427

Julius Caesar 4: 561

Junger, Sebastian 4: 694

K

Kaczynski, David 4: 590

Kaczynski, Theodore 4: 590

Kaiser, Henry John 2: 247

Kaiser, John 2: 247

Kamikaze at Leyte Gulf 3: 512–20, 514 (ill.), 518 (ill.)

Kasischke, Lou 1: 183

Kaufman, Irving 4: 639

Kefauver-Harris Act 2: 257

Kelsey, Frances Oldham 2: 256, 258

Kemeny Report 2: 300

Kemys, Lawrence 1: 45

Kennedy, John F. 2: 234, 257, 275; 3: 530, 531 (ill.), 534, 535, 537, 538; 4: 600

Kennedy, Robert F. 3: 540

Kerrigan, Nancy 4: 696, 700 (ill.), 701, 702

Keseberg, Lewis 1: 95

KGB 4: 675